ALBERT CAMUS

Modern Literature Monographs

ALBERT CAMUS

Carol Petersen

TRANSLATED BY ALEXANDER GODE

Frederick Ungar Publishing Co.
New York

Published by special arrangement with Colloquium Verlag, Berlin, publishers of the original German *Albert Camus*.

GM

~.~

By Way
of Introduction

The growing interest in Albert Camus, reflected in increasingly large printings of his works, bears witness
to this writer's ability to see the problems of contemporary life in sharp focus and to present them in a
manner significant to all of us. There was no literary
narcissism in him, no trace of the ambition of the
literato. The total absence in his works of any hint of
"art for art's sake," which was alien to his nature, is
doubtless a further reason for the enthusiastic readiness
particularly of the young both in France and abroad to
listen to him. He had and still has a wide circle of readers in the French working classes. His orientation both
as a writer and as a human being was in no sense determined by party politics. Propaganda, including the
"cultural" variety, was suspect to him, for he saw that

the coin of its realm—the catchword, the catchy phrase, and the slogan—is bound to be worn thin by daily use. This also won him numerous readers among those who were as unprejudiced as he was.

Yet the last secret of the breadth and depth of his appeal must, I think, be sought in the strength of his personality, which casts its spell on the reader the moment he takes up any one of Camus' works, whether it be a critical analysis of some question of the day, a reflection of his philosophical endeavor, or a product of his creative genius. The man Camus is present in every sentence he ever wrote. The man Camus, our fellowman, stands before us in full view and, as it were, within the reach of our handshake. The reader feels himself to be a partner, he feels that the venture—whatever it be—is a shared endeavor.

Whoever undertakes to write more or less comprehensively about Camus must therefore strive to do justice to the journalist, the philosophical thinker, and the creative author as triune aspects of a single person. To be sure, when such an undertaking has to respect preset limits of space, it is only natural that the presentation will stress the area in which Camus as a literary figure is bound to have the strongest effect, the area of social ethics, in which Camus—calmly yet unswervingly—displayed an eagerness to be fair, insofar as is humanly possible, to both friend and foe.

The foregoing considerations delineate the guiding principles of the present study. It was not my purpose to present a comprehensive survey of the life and the works of Camus; the limits of space would not have allowed such a broad study to become more than a two-dimensional map. To avoid this danger we had to over-look a considerable number of Camus' writings, espe-cially his journalistic output collected, in the original complete French edition of his works, in the three vol-umes of *Actuelles*. This made it possible to devote cor-respondingly greater attention to the author's untiring endeavor to cope, on the level of thought, with all the questions of life that kept coming into his purview.

As I found myself confronted with the totality of Camus' legacy, which although not voluminous is sig-nificant on many levels and extremely compressed in content, I took it to be my task to reveal its depth rather than to show its breadth and to use biographical data only to the extent that they could provide a frame for the resulting picture. Briefly, what guided me in the composition of this slim volume was the desire to give today's reader the feeling that he has met Albert Camus and to give a certain awareness of what the name, the work, and the life of Albert Camus signify in global terms, for he who has this awareness has in Albert Camus a guide and travel companion for his journey toward a better tomorrow.

C. P.

Contents

1

The Source

Si le langage de ces pays s'accordait
à ce qui résonnait profondément en moi,
ce n'est pas parce qu'il répondait à mes
questions, mais parce qu'il les rendait inutiles.[1]
[If the language of these lands was in harmony
with what reverberated deep within
me, the reason is not that it answered my
questions but that it made them superfluous.]

Whoever has had occasion to set foot on North African soil and has seen the glittering light under the clear blue, crystal-hard sky and the steeples and minarets of the white cities holds through his memories, as it were, a key that permits him immediate access to the character and the work of Albert Camus. For the gulf which the Mediterranean represents between the continents of Europe and Africa is wider and deeper than the noninitiate can readily understand. Indeed, in purely intellectual terms—without the help of sensuous experience—the significance of that gulf is difficult, if not impossible, to grasp.

To the end of his life Albert Camus remained faithful to his North African homeland, in particular the Algerian soil. He was born in Mondovi, a small village south of Bône, west of Oran, and east of Constantine. The date was November 7, 1913. His father, Lucien Camus, was a farmhand of Alsatian ancestry. His mother was a Spanish maid. Both parents had grown up as illiterates. In adult life, the father learned with great difficulty to read and write. The mother never did. She was hard of hearing and suffered from a speech impediment, both as aftermaths of a childhood illness that had not been properly cured. She was a woman of few words, to the point of leaving the impression that she was mute. There are in Albert Camus' works many moving passages that we can only read as descriptions of his mother, bearing witness to his deep-felt love for her. The following is such a passage.

"The boy's mother was silent too. When, as it would happen, she was asked, 'What are you thinking about?',

2

she replied, 'Nothing.' And that is the way it is. Everything is the way it is, and so there is nothing. Her life, her interests, her children are what they are, nothing more. They are there, that is all. It is not something to be felt. She was not very strong. It was difficult for her to think. She had a harsh and domineering mother who sacrificed everything to her animal egotism and who had for a long time held sway over the docile mind of her daughter. Marriage had set the daughter free, but when her husband died she came back, for that was what was expected of her. The husband, as the saying goes, had laid down his life for his country. His medals are still there, in a gilt frame, in a place for all to see. There is also a small shell splinter which was removed from his body. The army sent it to the soldier's widow. She has kept it. Her sorrow has long since gone. She has forgotten her husband, but she still speaks of the father of her children. To raise the children she goes out to work and gives the money she makes to her mother, who is taking care of raising the children. She does so with a whip. When she hits too hard, her daughter says to her: 'Don't hit their heads.' She loves her children because they are her children. She loves them with an impartial love that has never been expressed to them. Some evenings, he remembers them well, when she comes home from her exhausting work (she is a cleaning woman), she finds the house empty. Her mother has gone shopping, the children are still at school. She drops down in a chair, absorbed in gazing vacantly at some crack in the floor which she must follow. Around her darkness gathers in which this muteness is incurably disconso-

late. When the boy comes in at that moment, he sees the
bony shoulders, the emaciated outline of his mother's
figure. He stops, he is afraid. He begins to sense many
things. He has hardly come to be aware of his own existence. In the face of this animal silence he cannot weep.
He feels pity for his mother. Is that loving her? She has
never hugged and kissed him. She would not know how.
He stands there for minutes on end looking at her. He is
aware of standing apart and thus grows aware of how it
hurts. She does not hear him, she is quite deaf. In a
moment the old woman will come in. Life will begin
again: the cone of light of the petroleum lamp, the oil-
cloth on the table, the harsh voice, the vile words. But
meanwhile this silence marks a standstill of time, a
moment without measure. The boy vaguely senses these
things, and in their sensation, which pervades him, he
seems to sense that he feels love for his mother. That is
the way it should be. After all, she is his mother.

"She thinks of nothing. Outside it is still light. Outside there is the noise of the street. In here there is silence, silence in the night. The boy will grow up. He will
learn. He is being brought up, and he will be expected
to be grateful. As though he were shielded from pain.
His mother will always have her silences. He will keep
growing in pain. What counts is to be a man. His
grandmother will die, then his mother, then he." [2]

We have given this passage in full, for it will help
the reader to understand the figure of the mother in
Camus' work. The passage is a veiled description of
Camus' youth. It was intended to be a portrait of his
mother, an expression of his gratitude for her quiet,

self-sacrificing, and somehow mediating role. Camus' father had been killed one year after Albert's birth in the First Battle of the Marne in 1914, wearing the uniform of a Zouave. He was buried in a military cemetery in Brittany. Madame Camus took her two boys—Albert had a brother who was four years older and who grew up to make a living in the insurance business in Algiers—and moved to Belcourt, a crowded slum area of the Algerian capital. There she rented a two-room apartment in the Rue de Lyon which she shared with her mother and a half-paralyzed uncle of the children who was a barrelmaker.

To the end Camus never forgot or denied this world of calmly accepted silent poverty. On the contrary, even at the height of his fame, when he had achieved material security, he remembered it with pride and a sort of unconcealed happiness. To him, poverty under a Mediterranean sky, where an excess of warmth and sunlight somehow makes up for it, reducing it, restraining it, as it were, within bearable limits, was something quite different from the poverty which he came to know as a young man in the cities of continental Europe.

"I was born poor. I was born in a workman's quarter. But I did not know what misery was until I experienced the cold of our suburbs.[3] . . . In any event, the beautiful warmth that ruled over my childhood deprived me of all resentment. I lived a life of want but also, in a sense, of enjoyment. I felt within me unlimited powers. What was needed was merely that I should find the spot where they could be applied."[4]

These lines are quoted from the preface to the second edition (published in 1954) of Camus' earliest writings. Their purpose is made strikingly clear in the ensuing sentences, which sum up the essence of his early experience.

"Even the extreme wretchedness of the Arabs cannot be compared to the misery of the industrial suburbs. The skies above are different. Knowing the industrial suburbs, one feels tainted forever, I believe, and responsible for their existence." [5]

In 1918 Albert Camus began attending elementary school in Belcourt. He was no model boy in doing his daily lessons, but he got through the first six grades without difficulty, spending most of his leisure time at various sports. This life of emphasis on physical prowess, which he went on leading until a grave illness cast its first shadows on his adolescent years, echoes as part of a lost dream in his very last writings.

While he was still going to elementary school, Albert met for the first time a person ready and able to treat and respect him as a personality. This was his teacher Louis Germain, who evidently recognized even in those early days the boy's special gifts. It was through Germain's efforts that Albert was granted a scholarship enabling him at the age of ten to change over to the lycée. At first Madame Camus was suspicious of these developments, by instinct, as it were, sensing that this might lead to the alienation of her younger son. The teacher's insistence made her agree in the end, and so Albert was able to acquire a higher secondary-school education, which he accomplished again without scholastic difficulties, passing the university entrance examinations in

1932. The social differences of which the scholarship student at the lycée became aware during the years from 1923 to 1932 aroused in him, at least on occasion, a sense of rebellious discontent with the existing order of society and the corresponding order of values. But if this experience contributed to making Camus a critical and reflective young man, the event that caused him to mature early, raising him to a level far above that of his fellow students at the lycée in everything related to the questions of life and reality, was his first encounter with illness, his first encounter with death. In 1930, when he was only seventeen years old, he had his first serious attack of tuberculosis in the wake of an episode of pneumonia. Up to this time Albert had enjoyed excellent health. He had been much in demand as the goalkeeper of his rugby team, to which he had felt greatly attached and of which he had been an ever-popular member. Now for the first time an experience of weakness and helplessness was forced upon him. Since conditions at his home would not have allowed for proper treatment of his illness, he was taken to a hospital. Here, in the crowded ward of an impersonal public institution for the poor, misery in all its forms leaped at him from all around. This added a new dimension of depth to his social awareness both on the emotional and on the intellectual level, but, above all, it confronted him with the outlying border regions of human life delineated by bodily infirmity and man's helpless impotence. The year 1930 must thus be regarded in Camus' development as the beginning of a consciously and purposefully lived life. To call upon his contemporaries to join him in it came to be his special mission—one he never tired of to the end of his life.

After his discharge from the hospital, Camus did not return to his mother's home. For a short transitional period he stayed with an uncle of his, a butcher by trade, who lived under somewhat less meager circumstances. But then young Camus decided to live his own life in full independence.

This was a period of restlessness. Camus conceived the most varied plans for his future, but none of these seemed to satisfy him completely. He often changed his quarters, living alone at times and then in the company of friends of the same age group, but he never fell victim to idleness. He did not rest. The concentrated energy underlying all his activities commands respect. Considering the unsteady life he led, considering, too, that he had relinquished the last vestiges of bourgeois security, it is indeed amazing that he managed in 1932 to prepare for and pass his bachelor's examination. That very same year he took up the study of philosophy at the University of Algiers. It was again one of his teachers, this time at the lycée, who had showed him the way. This was the philosopher and man of letters Jean Grenier. Time and again, in the course of his later life, Camus expressed his sense of obligation and gratitude to Grenier, just as to his elementary-school teacher Germain. Camus' works stand, in a way, as an honoring monument to these men.

It seems as if Camus sensed at an early time that he was not to be granted a long life. What else can account for the fervor with which the newly matriculated student threw himself into the whirl of life at the university, (and not only at the university), in the Algiers of the 1930s? There was no work he considered too menial as long as it enabled him to live more intensely, to satisfy his growing demands on the life of the senses and of the spirit. He worked as an office clerk, as a salesman for automobile parts, as a meteorological helper, as a private tutor. In addition, he had begun to read systematically. Contemporary literature, in particular, began to exert an undeniable influence on him. There was Malraux, there was Montherlant, and above all there was André Gide—powerful at the time and commanding a larger following than any of the others. Their works and their personalities presented him with numerous problems which he could not and would not sidestep but which he tackled with characteristic passion. What impressed him most deeply time and again was the "asceticism of work." This meant to him, in his own words, "that there is no art and no greatness without the free acceptance of moral discipline." The most lasting effect on Camus at the time, however, came in the essays of his teacher, Grenier, which appeared under the title of *Les Iles* and in which the problems of existence were dealt with at once in a spirit of ironic skepticism and in poetic form. Camus' first published writings of 1937 bear witness to this influence. Then, too, the little-known novel *La Douleur*, by André de Richaud, must be mentioned at this point. Its setting was Algiers-Belcourt, a milieu thoroughly familiar to Camus. Its portrayals struck him as real and true to life. This work, if we may trust the appraisal made by Camus himself, was indeed one of the factors that made him definitively choose journalism—which he did in 1938—as his life's career.

Camus' personal life during his student days likewise took him to unusual heights—and depths. When he was only twenty years old he married Simone Hie, the daughter of an Algiers physician, but this marriage lasted only a little more than one year. There were no children.

"At Belcourt—just as at Bab-el-Oued—marriage comes early. Work comes very early, too, and in ten years the experience of a lifetime is lived out. At the age of thirty a worker has played all his trumps. He settles down to wait for the end, surrounded by his wife and his children. The happiness which he may have had has been keen and sudden. It has been merciless. So has his life. At that time a man comes to understand what it means to be born in this country where everything is given so that it may be taken away." [6]

It is important that we understand to what extent young Camus lived according to the laws of life of his native country. It is the law of the soil of North Africa which bids man live for and off the moment, without awareness of history or tradition, without forethought of the vital needs of tomorrow. The young who live on North African soil, whom the sky and the sea treat as their spoiled children, burn out their lives in lambent flames, and leave the future to fend for itself. They differ, not unimportantly, from the French of the European mother country in that they have unwittingly come to adopt in part the habits of life of the Mohammedans,

the Berbers, and Arabs who live around them. The line
drawn by the Mediterranean—this cannot be stated too
often—remains incalculable in its effects. Although
physical illness had undermined Camus' vital substance
in his early years, he remained to the end, in essence
and posture, a Frenchman of Algeria.

After his separation from Simone Hie, Camus took
a room with a view across the entire magnificent Bay of
Algiers. After the disappointment of his early marriage
he once again enjoyed the happy unconcern and cordial
comradeship of student life. The influence exerted on
him by Grenier as an artist and teacher remained great.
Over the years it came to be, if anything, still more decisive. "From Grenier I acquired the taste of a philosophical outlook." It was by way of Greek literature and
art that Grenier led his disciples to come to grips with
the problems of essence and existence, but he was one
of the fraternity of scholars to whom philosophical
thought can never be an end in itself. Insofar as philosophical probing could not contribute to a solution of
the problems of the day he regarded it as barren and
vain. He thought little of abstractions whose worth
could not be confirmed in the personal experience of
factual reality. It is only natural that such an intellect
made a particularly deep impression on a young man
such as Camus, whose passionate endeavor both on the
intellectual and on the spiritual plane was dedicated to
the active service of life and the living; and far beyond
his student years Camus thought of Grenier as a mentor
and master. The teacher-disciple relationship which
linked the two survived intact the strain of Camus' deci-

sion late in 1934 to join the Communist Party. Grenier must have understood that the leftist radicalism of the time—characterized as it was, in bearing and outlook, by its advocacy of world brotherhood—was naturally congenial to the quest of experience of his twenty-one-year-old friend and student. On the other hand, Camus' step was also in keeping with the trend of the times— one might. say, with the fashion of the day—which proved sufficiently powerful to conquer, at least for a while, a mind as extreme in its individualistic bend as that of André Gide. About one year later, in 1935, Camus left the Party again, after Foreign Minister Laval's trip to Moscow had resulted in modifications of the Communist Party line regarding the Moslem demands which Camus considered justified and which he wished to back and see backed.

In 1936 Camus began the actual writing of his philosophical thesis. It dealt with the relations of Hellenism and Christianity in Plotinus and Saint Augustine. This was indeed a remarkable subject, considering that young Camus felt rather remote from the Church and any kind of Church dogma and had far preferred to live his life in accordance with the hedonistic precepts of a religion of nature. Nonetheless his presentation was extremely successful. It would seem that Camus' endeavor to find his own philosophical style gave him a very strong urge to work his way through systems of thought that were alien to him. We may well see in this an early reflection of Camus' inveterate striving to do justice to all phenomena of life, to all phenomena of the spirit, and to be objective in their presentation. In terms of this goal, which he was to achieve to an exceptionally high degree, no better training could be imagined than that represented by the discipline of long years of philosophical studies. There is, simultaneously, the important fact that the French culture tradition establishes intimate links between philosophical scholarship and literature in the sense of *belles lettres*. It is in keeping with this that throughout his student years Camus commuted, as it were, between the two fields, which proved to be a boon to his later work in the area of his true calling, that is to say, the field of the philosophical essay.

There was a third area in which Camus was active with great success. This was the theater, in which his efforts date back as far as 1935, that is to say, to the time shortly after he had left the Communist Party. "The tall young man, slender and pale, passionate, indefatigable in spite of his illness"—to describe Camus with the words used by Blanche Balain, a member of the company of which he was to be the center during the years from 1937 to 1939—seemed to be so full of drive, so parched with thirst for life, that he could not resist taking an active part in all manifestations of cultural endeavor. This does not exclude a second possible interpretation—that Camus was a man who could not derive full satisfaction from living and working in isolation. It is quite possible that his boyhood interest in sports was motivated by the fact that his school and home tasks did not provide the fullness of life he needed, and thus only the atmosphere of team comradeship allowed him to deploy and employ his strengths.

Perhaps, too, his short-lived membership in the Communist Party was proof that group work alone could stimulate him to the highest excellence of performance. A man like Camus who, when among men, was first and foremost a comrade—and hardly anyone who ever knew him has failed to mention this fact with pleasure and gratitude—could not achieve a feeling of fulfillment in the exclusive isolation and aloofness of artistic creation.

The fourth decade of this century was characterized by a spreading awareness of political responsibility. In France this trend was decisively accelerated by the prevailing leftist orientation of the intellectuals and the countless German refugees of the Hitler era. In Algeria, too, the resulting sociopolitical climate was favorable to the development of a close collaboration between politicians and artists. Individual workmen, and hence the working classes as such, had long since come to play an integral part in literary production, but now it occurred more and more as a matter of course that men and women who had come up from the working proletariat were called upon to assume active functions and positions in their country's cultural life. Camus, who fit this description perfectly, was alertly conscious of the distinguishing characteristics of the age. In response to the call of the hour, in 1935 in Algiers he founded the *Théâtre du Travail,* which survived for four years. The members of this company were by no means professional actors but exclusively students and workers. The theater opened after the publication of a manifesto written by Camus himself.

"In Algiers," the text said in part, "the establishment of a workmen's theater has been accomplished as a dedicated collective endeavor. This theater, conscious of the artistic values contained in the literature of the masses, wishes to prove that it may be beneficial to art if on occasion it is made to leave its ivory tower. This theater claims that the sense of beauty is inseparably linked to a certain sense of humanity. . . . Its objective is to impart new vitality to certain human values but not to present new ideological systems. . . ."[7]

It was not long before Camus was made to understand that much of this program for the future was to fall by the wayside through the corrective intervention of life's vicissitudes. The first offering of the new theater was a pronounced success. The play was a dramatized version of Malraux's short novel *Le Temps du mépris*, which deals with the experiences and reactions of a German Communist leader who has spent tormenting days in solitary confinement in a Gestapo prison but then is given a chance to escape by plane to Prague because a comrade of his, assuming his name, has sacrificed himself in his stead. It may have been the timeliness of the theme that cast its spell on the audience, but it may also have been, quite simply, the passionate candor of its presentation. In those days little was known throughout the world of the atrocities which had come to be matters of routine in the Germany of 1935. The full truth was known only in extremely well-informed circles, of the kind which Camus spared no effort to join.

It was in the same spirit that in 1936, immediately after the outbreak of the Spanish Civil War, Camus,

striking while the iron was hot, wrote with his fellows the
collective four-act play *Révolte dans les Asturies* on an
uprising of mineworkers which had been beaten down
by brute force two years previously in Oviedo. The play
is the only extant piece of teamwork produced by the
Théâtre du Travail. It was printed but not performed.
The municipal authorities were worried about the reactions it might provoke. There was no objection to the
theater as a forum of just social proclamation, but the
theater as a rostrum for political agitation was a different matter. Basically Camus himself even then was inclined to think of the theater primarily as an institution
for the presentation of human values—of man's innocence, which it is possible for men to preserve even
though they live in times of catastrophe—and so he
agreed to the cancellation of the scheduled performance
of *Révolte dans les Asturies*. The work of the *Théâtre du
Travail* continued under the name *Théâtre de l'Equipe*.
From now on plays previously performed elsewhere, including some from the literature of the nineteenth century, were taken into the repertory. A stage version of
Dostoevski's *The Brothers Karamazov*, in which Camus
played the part of Ivan, was generally regarded as the
high point in the life of this small theater which rapidly
achieved recognition and renown. It was at this time
that Camus thought for the first time of preparing in a
similar way a stage version of Dostoevski's *The Demons*, but this plan materialized only in 1959.

Camus' enthusiasm for the theater was by no means
a short-lived infatuation. To the time of his death he was
actively involved in stage work in various cities of
France, particularly in Paris. The plays which he him-

self contributed to European dramatic literature will be taken up in a later context. Here, however, we may note that shortly before his death Camus was promised the directorship of a theater of his own in Paris by André Malraux, who had meanwhile become Minister for Cultural Affairs of the Fifth Republic.

In 1937 Camus suffered another violent relapse of his illness. This prevented him from taking his oral state examination, but we may assume that he was ready to take the disappointment in stride. After all, he had proved himself in various areas of life, and his roster of successes—although he was only twenty-four years old—was already impressive. In the same year, 1937, he also laid the foundations for his renown as a writer. Edmond Charlot, a publisher in Algiers, brought out a first collection of literary essays written by Camus. The title was *L'Envers et l'endroit*. When he was offered a teaching position at the lycée of Sidi-bel-Abbès, he felt that he could afford to turn down the opportunity because he feared that a position of this kind, and its exacting routine, would force him into a rut and make him lose his receptive alertness to all the multiple aspects of life. Instead, late in the summer of 1937 he went to Savoy to rest from his prolonged illness for a few months, to be in the quiet world of the mountains where he could think over his life once again in order to be ready to start out again under the law which was to be the law of his life to the very end. It demanded of him that he acknowledge himself to be "a servant of truth and a servant of freedom." This—as he said himself—was the greatness of his calling as an artist.

2

In the Foothills of Knowledge

*Il n'y a pas d'amour de vivre
sans désespoir de vivre.*[1]
[There is no love of life
without despair of life.]

In the preface to Camus' collected literary essays, published in their definitive version in 1954, there are two eminently characteristic passages.

"In my innermost heart," reads the one, "I feel humble only before the lives of the poorest or before the great ventures of the spirit. In between, there is today a society that makes me laugh." [2]

The second quotation, from the same preface, is this: "Solitude reunites those whom society separates." [3]

In these utterances we clearly recognize the position which Camus consciously took in his activity as a writer. The center of his interest is man as a sensing and acting being, independent of his social role and the functions it imposes on him. Camus' concern is man at the mercy of the powers of nature, man in fear of being overpowered by something, man in the face of death, man in the utter loneliness of his hopeless, defenseless exposure.

In Camus' first five essays, which represent the literary harvest of the years 1935 and 1936, we characteristically meet men and women who are, in one sense or another, *in extremis*, who find themselves at the confines of life, in a situation at the edge of the abyss from which there is no salvation and no redemption. They must recognize that they are strangers on this earth, that they have never really been anything else. In the essay bearing the title *L'Ironie* there is an old woman left alone by her visitor because he wants to go to the movies; there is an old man whom the young abandon while "in the evening of his life age befalls him as recurrences of nausea" [4]; finally, there is a grandmother whose hard, bitter death her grandchildren take in stride. Three destinies which touch the reader directly, just because they are so plain, just because they are everyday occurrences of a kind no one can fail to understand. But death, when it comes, does not have the effect of a gentle redemption. It is the consistent exit from such strangeness, a consistent seal on a destiny so lived, for which there is no solace, for which there is and for which there can be no solace. The poor know this better than the wealthy, for the wealthy—throughout their lives—are accustomed to concealing strangeness and solitude on earth behind vestments of illusory and deceitful hopes.

It might seem at first that Camus did nothing here but record simple facts, conditions of the kind that his youth, spent in the world of poverty, had shown him day in and day out. Yet—even if we were without the key phrase from the preface subsequently written by Camus and quoted by us as the epigraph of this chapter in order to avoid undue and exclusive reliance on our subjective interpretation—it seems impossible that anyone should fail to sense the restrained emotion that oppresses the author. As one reads on in Camus' works, on and on to the end, one recognizes ever more clearly—as a specific characteristic, as a tendency clearly discernible now (in retrospect from a later vantage point) even in his earliest attempts—that in all his creative efforts he would start out from elements in his personal experience, striving relentlessly in the course of the work to free himself from this experience, "to get away from it," and to achieve an artistic form progressively more impersonal, or better, depersonalized, in character. The three sketches of old age presented in the essay *L'Ironie* are summed up in a one-paragraph reflective afterword in which, as it were, Camus expressly disavowed any kind of subjective involvement in these destinies through personal recollection. This, it seems to me, is a particularly clear expression of Camus' depersonalizing bent, possibly not in spite of but because of the fact that this little afterword in all its directness still indicates a certain stylistic immaturity and indeed helplessness. From the very beginning Camus strove to master the stylistic device of irony for the sake of distance and detachment, and the title chosen for the three sketches appears to be significant and symptomatic.

"All that," asks the afterword, "does not gibe? Who said it did? A woman left alone for the sake of the movies, an old man no one any longer listens to, a death which makes up for nothing, and then—turning around —all the light of the world. What difference does it make if one accepts it all? There are here three destinies which are alike and yet different. Death for all, but to each his own. After all, the sun can be relied upon to keep our bones warm." [5]

The figure of the mother, the grandmother, or the old woman generally, is a kind of leitmotiv in Camus' work as a whole. This makes it time and again emphatically clear how deeply and lastingly the author's mother and grandmother—each in her own way—affected him during his childhood. His second essay, *Entre oui et non*, is dominated by this very figure. The core of the action, as holds true for most of Camus' prose works, is minimal. There is hardly more than a night watch kept by a son at the bedside of his fever-stricken mother, with a few scant spoken words but—to make up for it—very extended reflections on the part of the young man. Once again, it is abundantly clear, Camus evokes his childhood home as a setting.

"Evenings, in summertime, the workmen sit on their 'balconies.' Where he lived there was only a very small window. Chairs were then carried down outside the house where one could enjoy the evening. There was the street, ice vendors next door, cafés on the other side, and the noise of children running from door to door.[6] . . . At midnight the last streetcar took with it every remaining hope that comes to us from human life, all the reassurance we derive from the noise of cities. The house was filled, just one more time, with the echo of the passing trolley. Then, gradually, all died down. There was nothing left but a vast garden of silence and growing in it here and there a fear-filled moan from the sick woman. He had never felt so lost. The world had dissolved and with it the illusion that life begins anew every day." [7]

It may have been in hours such as these that Camus learned to look steadfastly and clearly into the face of his destiny. What accounts for the great and profound impression left on us even by this early piece of prose is, in full keeping with the factual situation, the clarity and unambiguous precision of the writer's statement. This precision Camus managed to preserve even in the aloofness of his later abstractions. A man to whom hardship and scarcity are familiar from his early years has learned to "look closely," and whoever has learned to look closely and clearly will—if there is a poet in him— be clear and precise in the use of words. No one will doubt that this applies to Camus after the passages just quoted.

In 1937 Camus for the first time left his Algerian homeland. He traveled throughout Europe, visiting Czechoslovakia, Austria, Italy, and the Balearic Islands, and gathered proof and confirmation of his world outlook and his conception of the essence and the value of life. In the course of these weeks and months the receptive young man did more than widen his horizon in the ordinary sense. It was not Camus' objective to relax; still less did he travel to satisfy a desire to find diversion or pleasure. What motivated him was clearly the urge— initially no doubt unconscious and unknown to himself —to come to a better understanding of his own being by exposing it to an unfamiliar environment. For the sake of this objective he was ready to accept inconvenience, loneliness, and indeed desolate fear. He was out to test whether the world beyond the accustomed confines would or would not agree with the meaningfulness of his own existence. The third of the essays in this early collection, *La Mort dans l'âme*, is a statement of Camus' first travel experiences. Prague, which was his first stop, was to him a piece of alien and hostile life that wanted none of him. In the figure of the dead man whom he saw through an open door, lying on a hotel bed, the true significance of his visit to Prague came to be epitomized: the encounter with death, which tends to be particularly impressive away from home.

"The hotel staff in the hall were whispering. I quickly went upstairs not to delay being face to face with what I expected. I had been right. The door to the room was ajar and nothing could be seen through it but a bare wall that was painted blue. The dull light that had struck me before projected on this screen the shadow of a man stretched out on a bed and that of a policeman standing guard over the body. The two shadows intersected at right angles. It was the light that disconcerted me. It was real enough, the real light of life, of an afternoon of life, a light that makes one feel one is alive. Yet that man was dead. Alone in his room. I knew he had not killed himself. I hurried back to my room and threw myself down on my bed. A man like many another, small and heavy, to judge by his shadow. He had doubtless been dead for a long time. Life at the hotel had gone on until it occurred to the bellboy to look for him. He had arrived here in unsuspecting naïveté, and he died alone. I—at that time—was reading the package insert of my shaving cream. I spent the entire afternoon in a state which I would have difficulty describing. I lay stretched out; my head was empty; my heart felt strangely oppressed. I did my fingernails. I counted the joints in the wooden floor. 'If I can count up to one thousand. . . .' At fifty or sixty I stopped. I could not go on." [8]

Although "the walls of Prague" seemed to choke him, in Italy, where Camus turned next, he saw himself again in the accustomed flood of light. He again felt that he was "facing the world," learning simultaneously, however, that this recovered peace was still not more than a "peace without joy," a "fulfillment without tears." The shadow of the dead in Prague had come with him, never to leave him again.

"The sun had almost reached the highest point in the sky, and the sky was of a keen yet airy blue. The mass of light poured out by the sky came rolling down the slopes of the hills investing in robes of heat the cypress and olive trees and the white houses and their red roofs, to go on losing itself in the plains steaming with sun. And time and again the same nakedness. Within me the horizontal shadow of the stout and heavy little man. In the plains writhing in the sun and the dust, in the denuded hills all covered with scorched vegetation, whatever I touched with my fingers was a stripped, peeled form of the taste of nothingness that I carried within myself. This land took me back to the core of my being and made me face my own anxiety. And it was and was not the anxiety of Prague. How shall I explain it? It remains a fact that in the face of this Italian plain peopled with trees, sun, and smiles I grasped better than anywhere else the odor of death and inhumanity that had been pursuing me throughout the last months. . . . [9]

"For me there was no promise of immortality in this country. What is it that made me, without eyes to see, relive Vicenza in my soul, without hands to touch, the raisins of Vicenza, without a skin to feel, the caress of the night on the road from Monte Berico to Villa Valmarana? [10]

"I should say I often return to Prague and the deadly days I lived through there. I have found my city again. At times, though, a sharp odor of cucumbers and vinegar reawakens my unease. I then force myself to think of Vicenza. Yet both are dear to me and I have trouble separating my love of light and life from my secret devotion to the experience of despair that I have tried to describe. . . ." [11]

When Camus formulated this thought for the first time, when for the first time he recognized within himself its truth, he had once and for all found his position: his viewpoint, in the full sense of the locus from which he was destined to look out on life. To know what this position was is indispensable if we wish to understand any of his later utterances. "There is no love of life without despair of life." With this established, it is, at best, of secondary importance where the traveler turned his steps next, for the experiences we derive from our travels are in their substance everywhere and at all times the same; they are phenomenal replicas of primordial experiences which man endeavors to attain in the depths of his being, even though education and optimistic civility will in many instances interfere. Simultaneously they are experiences that cannot be taught or be taken over from others. They become our own and can enrich us only after we have found them ourselves.

With this knowledge Camus opened up for himself the gates to the highest possible degree of inner freedom. Nature around him and the sky above are without significance for a man's destiny. They have no bearing on it. It was only now, when his travels had given him this insight, that Camus could begin to give his life a shape that was truly his own. A man is really free only when he is himself the foundation on which he stands,

when he has learned to dispense with all irrational sup-
ply lines to the rear. Camus traveled on, he traveled to
Majorca, to Iviza, only now truly imbued with "love of
life." And *Amour de vivre* is indeed the title of the
fourth essay of the series, "for the blessing of travel is
fear." [12]

"The blessing of travel is fear. It breaks up within
us a sort of inner décor. We have lost every possibility
of cheating, of hiding behind office hours or shop time
(against which we protest so strenuously and yet without which we have no defense against the tremorous experience of being alone). This explains why I keep
wishing to write novels in which my heroes would say:
'What would I do without my hours at the office?' Or
again: 'My wife has died but luckily I have a fat pile of
papers to work up for tomorrow.' Travels deprive us of
this escape. Far away from family and friends, far away
from our language, gone away from all our supports,
deprived of our masks (we do not know the streetcar
fare, and everything is like that), we are entirely at the
surface of ourselves. But there is also this: As we sense
that our souls are sick, we restore to every being, to
every object its status of miracle. A woman dancing
without thought of anything, a bottle on a table seen
behind a curtain: every picture turns into an image. All
of life appears to be symbolized by it to the extent that
our own lives are summed up in it at this particular
moment. We are receptive to all gifts. There is no way
of describing the contradictory experiences of drunken-
ness of which we are able to partake (including that of
lucidity). No country away from the Mediterranean, it

seems, has taken me simultaneously so far away from myself and so close to me." [13]

What Camus experienced in the course of this journey was more and more an expanded view of the world with man's role in it abstracted, comparable to the experience the Engadine had once meant to Nietzsche: "The world is deeper than the day may think." It was, in fact, in 1938 that Camus began to concern himself seriously with Nietzsche. In any event, he summarized his first "Mediterranean" experience—made conscious through the earlier European journey—in this realization:

"For, after all, what struck me then was not a world made after the measure of man but one closing up over man. No, if the language of these lands was in harmony with what reverberated deep within me, the reason is not that it answered my questions but that it made them superfluous. It was not thanksgiving that could rise to my lips but the *nada* which could not have been borne but in the sight of lands which are crushed by the sun. There is no love of life without despair of life." [14]

In the final essay in this first, not at all widely disseminated collection, the title essay *L'Envers et l'endroit*, Camus returned once again to the distinctive fate of man in old age. We are told of the woman who uses a certain sum of money she has inherited to purchase for herself "a sumptuous burial vault, sober of line, in black marble" [15] and proceeds to have her name engraved in gold lettering on the gravestone. Once this is accomplished, she spends every Sunday afternoon in her vault repeating over and over again a rite signifying the juxtaposition of what she is with what she is going to be, with the remarkable result that one day she actually understands that she is dead in the eyes of the world. At the same time, elsewhere, there is a man in his room watching the play of the sunlight on the window curtains, with the result that a boundless joy of life begins to reverberate in him. The two, Camus intimates, are opening their eyes to the same reality.

"Courage, great courage is to keep our eyes open to light and to keep them open to death. Beyond that, there is no way of speaking of the link between this devouring love of life and this secret despair. If I listen to Irony in her hiding place at the bottom of things (this guarantor of freedom, as Barrès called her), she slowly uncovers herself, winks at me from a bright little eye and says 'Live as though. . . .' Despite all my searching, that is the sum of my wisdom." [16]

This "as-though" affirmation of life, born from the knowledge that life is doubtless irrational and not within the range of logical understanding, identifies Camus' standpoint at the threshold of his twenty-fifth year. Life and death are equally incomprehensible to us, and yet what is demanded of us is not only to accept them both patiently but to acknowledge and affirm them in their entire potential weight. The endeavor to understand the secret of life and death is meaningless and condemned in advance to failure. The procedure cannot possibly yield a fruitful result. On the contrary, it might interfere in our tacit accord with our fellow beings. To what extent this accord mattered to Camus, to what extent he considered it crucial, has already been amply stated. In the course of Camus' later development, it came to be ever more exclusively the one prominent value; he made this accord the center of all his endeavors and wished to see it become the center of the endeavors of all men.

Only one year after the publication of the essays just discussed, Camus surprised his friends in Algeria (outside of which he had hardly more than a handful of readers at the time) with a sort of second installment that was likewise brought out by his friend, the publisher Charlot in Algiers. This second collection, released in 1938, contained only four essays, which are really nothing but a paean to life and the abundance of its possibilities and to a free humanity. In a sense Camus celebrated in these essays the world he had newly discovered through the pitiless experiences of his European journey. Never again shall we hear Camus' voice jubilate as exuberantly as in these four prose pieces. They represent, as it were, the irrevocable marriage of the Mediterranean Camus, as the North African coastal region had molded him, with the soil of his native land. They constitute Camus' definitive title to all the forces which shaped and preserved that land and which henceforth, since they were his in heightened and conscious awareness, he could never again lose, regardless of where the vicissitudes of his career might place him. It is doubtless no accident that the collective title chosen for these essays was *Noces*. They are "impressions on the edge of the desert," and only the fourth and last essay takes us back once again to Italy, particularly to Florence, perhaps only to demonstrate how even there salvation cannot be looked for outside this world and that it is this world which Florentine "hymns of stone" succeed in making beautiful.

Never again was Camus to look as painstakingly at a landscape, never again was he to allow himself as much room to become himself a part of it, as he did in these four essays. Two localities, Tipasa and Djémila, are the center from which he spread out the riches of his earth and the people living on it. Tipasa and Djémila are two towns that still have ruins of Roman buildings, although these mean little to the present inhabitants, who live on the whole without awareness of history and precisely for that reason the more fully, the more truly. *Noces à Tipasa,* the first of the four essays, has no other theme except the joy of being alive on this earth and of accomplishing on it a task as a human being.

"I leave to others now all thought of order and restraint. The vast excesses of nature and the sea have taken hold of my entire being. In this marriage of ruins and spring, the ruins have become stones again, have lost the finish wrought in them by human hands, have found their way back into nature. To celebrate the return of her prodigal children nature prodigally put forth her flowers. Between the flat stones of the forum heliotropes hold up their round white heads, and red geraniums pour their blood on what were once houses, temples, and public places. As there are men whom much knowledge leads back to God, so does much time lead the ruins back to the house of their mother.[17]

"Happy the living on this earth who have seen these things. Seen, seen on this earth. How can one forget? At the Eleusinian mysteries it was enough to ponder. Here I ponder and know that I shall never be close enough to this world. I want to be naked, want to throw myself into the waves and bathe in them the fragrant essences of earth with which I am still wholly imbued, to accomplish on my skin the embrace which, lip to lip, has for so long been all that earth and sea were craving.[18]

"I love this life without restraint and wish to speak of it in full abandon. It teaches me how to be proud of my human state. Yet, I have often been told, there is nothing to be proud of. But there is. There is the sun, this sea, my heart thumping with youth, my body tasting of salt, and the immense setting in which tenderness and glory merge in yellow and blue. To make that my own I shall muster my strength and my reserves. Here nothing makes me what I am not. I relinquish no part of myself. I don no mask. It is enough that I patiently learn the difficult craft of living which readily outweighs other people's know-how of life." [19]

In this description Camus lavishes his descriptive powers on his subject with a virtually Dionysian sweep. The second essay, *Le Vent à Djémila*, is by comparison more reflective, more concerned once again with the writer's lonely humanity. Is it the city of ruins that made him think of death? This is not the first time he comes face to face with death; yet somehow there has been in his awareness of nonlife an element of casual acquaintance. Djémila bestowed on him a clear knowledge of the inescapability of death which, however, man will meet in greater dignity if he does so consciously and at the same time in full acceptance of the fact that death will signify his irrevocable extinction.

"It affords me no satisfaction to believe that death marks the beginning of another life. Death to me is a locked door. It is not, I say, a threshold to be crossed. I say it is an event that will come. It is horrible and unclean. All the relevant arguments I have been offered strive to rid man of the burden of his own life. As I see great birds fly heavily through the sky over Djémila, it is precisely a certain burden of life that I demand and that I am given. To be unbroken in this passive passion on the cross. The rest is not for me. There is in me too much youth, and I cannot speak of death. But it seems to me that if I had to speak of death, it is here that I would find the right words between horror and silence, to speak of the conscious certitude of a death without hope.[20]

"Djémila . . . , and I sense clearly now that the true, the only progress of civilization—which a man from time to time attains—consists in the creation of conscious deaths.[21]

"The creation of conscious deaths reduces the distance which separates us from the world, enables us—without joy—to wind up in conscious remembrance of the exalting images of a world lost to us forever. And the sad song of the hills of Djémila embeds the bitterness of this lesson more deeply in my soul." [22]

Camus' attitude toward death is that of a man who has severed all links to Christianity. Beyond first communion he took no part in the life of the Church. Later on he explicitly called himself an atheist. We shall see in due time how, in times of need, he nonetheless proved himself in the spirit of true love of neighbor in his dealings with his fellow men. It is also true, as we shall see, that his last great prose work again made use at least of a Christian "notation." For the time being Christian values—the division of human acts and reactions into good and evil—were of no great concern to him. Intellectual speculation beyond death struck him as idle. In *L'Eté à Alger,* the third essay in the present collection, he wrote:

"It is the truths which are relative that alone touch me. The others, the ideal ones, I cannot understand for lack of soul. Not that we should play at being animals, but I have no taste for the state of bliss of angels. I merely know that the sky will outlast me. And what else can I mean by eternity but that which goes on after my death? [23]

"There are words that I have never really understood, such as the word 'sin.' I am convinced, however, that these men [of Belcourt] have not sinned against life. For, if there is a sin against life, it is likely that it consists not so much in despairing of life as in hoping for another and in escaping the implacable grandeur of this one." [24]

This conception of life, which has its own distinctive rigors, appeared to Camus to find corroboration of its legitimacy in Italian art, particularly in the art of Florence. In the fourth and last essay of this collection, *Le Désert,* Camus exclaimed:

"Florence! One of the rare places in Europe where I have understood that dormant at the core of my rebellion lies an assent. In its sky, in which tears and sun mingle, I learned to give my assent to the earth and to burn in these somber flames of its feasts." [25]

And again: "But it must also be understood that I

say 'truth' only in order to consecrate a higher poetry: the black flame which Italian painters, from Cimabue to Francesca, have lit throughout the landscapes of Tuscany as a lucid protest of man cast upon an earth whose splendor and light speak to him relentlessly of a god that does not exist." [26]

Camus himself would not have been able to say whether he derived these insights from Italy or directly from his own heart. Yet the fact that, in a world of such splendor as Italy and its art, men have always died and always will die seemed to confirm his conviction that there are no truths other than truths that must perish.

Who would deny that the abundant imagery and the wealth of thought of these two collections of essays (of which we have not been able to give more than a weak reflection) are truly unequaled and may well be called overwhelming? We sense the vast vitality of their author pulsing through them. And this in fact raises the question whether these pieces are really essays in the sense in which we usually understand that term. Is there not too great a preponderance of rhetorical pronouncement in them, too strong an element of critical analysis? I am inclined to think that all of Camus' early writings reveal an immanent tendency to become "poetry in prose" in a spirit of strongly secularized mysticism. Indeed, it is a historical fact that questions of aesthetic form began to concern Camus seriously only when he tried his hand at writing for the stage.

Camus' first play, *Caligula,* had its premiere only in 1945, but it was written in 1938. It was originally intended for the *Théâtre de l'Equipe,* and Camus himself planned to play the part of the insane emperor at the premiere. Things did not work out that way. Camus had become interested in the subject while reading Suetonius' *Lives of the Caesars,* but the execution of the plan became unwittingly more exacting and broader in its dimensions than lay actors could have handled with any hope of achieving the kind of success Camus had a right to expect, that is, the kind of success the play did in fact attain seven years later at the Théâtre Hébertot in Paris with Gérard Philippe in the title role.

Caligula, the third emperor of Rome, succeeding Tiberius to the throne, had known throughout the early years of his rule how to make himself popular with both the masses and the Senate. After the death of his sister and mistress he realized that the world, by its nature and essence, is inadequate. "Men die and are not happy," was the lesson which he derived from days of aimless wandering about and with which he returned to his palace, a wholly different man, as his environment was soon to learn with horror and dismay. If the world is meaningless and bad, nothing—he concluded—can be forbidden, for everything is devoid of significance. He begins to live in accordance with this precept, instituting a rule of terror, "denying friendship and love, good and evil, the simple community of men," pronounces death sentences at the whim of the moment, and finally demands for himself—the moon. Driven to establish on earth the rule of the absurd, he is going to teach men to stop being deceived by false rational arguments. He denies once and for all the existence of the gods, overlooking, to be sure, that this denial implies that he is simultaneously denying the existence of men. While sowing the seeds of boundless hate, he fails to see that in doing so he delivers into the hands of those around him more and more weapons which they can use to kill him as a victim of their lust for murder. "A suicide on a higher plane," as Camus himself put it, making evident the tragic error involved in the conclusion that being true to ourselves may, under certain conditions, justify our being untrue in our obligations to our fellow men. If there is a lesson here it is clearly that man cannot attain freedom at the expense of those around him.

In the preface which Camus wrote for the 1959 edition of his collected plays, he emphasized that in writing *Caligula* he was not motivated by the desire to "shock." This kind of sensationalism is something of which Camus was totally incapable. What he wished to achieve was rather a demonstration of the devastating consequences of the lack of restraint, of the hubris of men which he witnessed coming to the fore, particularly under the dictatorships of his day and age. When Camus wrote this play, Hitler was not yet in France. Indeed, it anticipated conditions which but a few years later were to become cruel reality. When after the Second World War *Caligula* began to be performed in the theaters throughout the world, this "tragedy of reason" was readily understood. Of all of Camus' stage plays, *Caligula* was destined to become the most successful.

This detour into history enabled Camus to speak more directly to his contemporaries. This was indeed fully consistent with the objectives implied in his own development. He became increasingly aware of the urgency and seriousness of his calling in the political arena of the day. In the same year in which *Caligula* was written, that is, in 1938, Camus accepted the invitation to work for the socialist newspaper *Alger Républicain*. This was no particularly remunerative activity. The paper was at all times faced with serious economic difficulties. If Camus, nonetheless, kept up this work with steadfast dedication—facing slander and, at the end of two years, the forced removal from his post—it was because it gave him a welcome chance to draw attention to the wretched conditions which the Algerian policies of the French government of those years had allowed to develop in his native land and to expose the men principally responsible for them. Pascal Pia, the founder and editor of the paper—a physically massive and intellectually subtle journalist and human being— came to be an intimate friend of Camus. The genuine strength of this relationship was to be given many a chance to prove itself when the two men worked together as members of the resistance movement. In the summer of 1939 Camus' paper (fighting for its life in unequal competition with the conservative and conformist *Echo d'Alger*) sent him into the mountains south of Algiers, where he was to study the living conditions of the Kabyle people, who were passing through a grave economic crisis. The human misery and suffering Camus witnessed in the course of this mission surpassed everything he had known so far. In ten major newspaper articles Camus described in detail the subhuman conditions he had found. These articles (now available

as part of Camus' *Chroniques algériennes, 1938–1958*)
are still worth reading. The factual information on
which they were based can be verified and is of historical significance. Beyond that, there is an unmistakable
overtone of the ever-present, profound, and strong sen-
sitivity of the writer in the face of human suffering.
This imparts to these reports, unintentionally, a significance that far exceeds their informational value. Indeed, they are eminently fit to help us establish a very
intimate personal acquaintanceship with the man Albert Camus.

After the hardships of these quasi-official travels
through virtually uncharted territory (with little possibility of being heedful of his still precarious health),
Camus made plans to spend a few weeks of vacation in
Greece. The events of the day interfered. He canceled
his steamer reservation and held himself in readiness
for new assignments in the service of his times.

3

~.

The World
of the Absurd

Le ver se trouve au coeur de l'homme.[1]
[The worm is in the heart of man.]

Instead of sailing toward the land of his dreams, Camus volunteered for military service in the very first days of September 1939. This is surprising. Young Camus, in his overall demeanor, had been anything but soldierly. Part of his motivation to take this step may have been the disappointment with military censors whom the government appointed to control the editorial tenor of his newspaper, an event which resulted in the exclusion of Camus from the responsible editors by reason of his eyebrow-raising and, indeed, aggressive, even rebellious, series of articles on the wretched conditions prevailing among the Kabyles. Another significant point may have been Camus' desire to show his solidarity with those millions of his equals in age and fate who were being drawn on both sides into the bloodiest of adventures. But let us listen to Camus himself:

"It is always senseless to dissociate oneself from others, even from their stupidity and cruelty. We cannot pretend: 'That is none of my concern.' We are in the fight against it or for it. Nothing is less excusable than war and the appeal to national hate. But once war has come, it is useless and cowardly to stand aside and to pretend: 'I am not responsible.' The ivory towers have collapsed. There is no sparing ourselves, for there is no sparing the others."

It was almost a disappointment to Camus that he was excluded from military service because of his tubercular susceptibility. He had not wanted to stand aside while the events of wartime subjected all life to a new, incomparably harder law. There were as yet no national or patriotic impulses in what induced him to try to sign

up. It was much more an expression of his instinctive
awareness of being a member of the human fellowship.
When the decision thwarting his desire seemed irrevocable, he could only accept it, and since there was little
he could do to make a living in Algiers, he went to Oran,
where he stayed for a short time until his friend Pascal
Pia got him a job as reporter on the Paris newspaper
Paris-Soir.

After the occupation of Paris by the German army
in May 1940, *Paris-Soir,* like other papers in the capital,
moved to the as yet unoccupied portion of France. The
place chosen was Clermont-Ferrand. However, Camus
stayed there with the paper for only a short while before
relocating in Lyons. It was during this time that he
married for a second time. His wife was a young
Frenchwoman, Francine Faure, a native of Oran. With
her Camus moved to her native city in January 1941,
no doubt because the climate and the atmosphere of the
industrial cities of the Auvergne and of Lyons were bad
for his health (and also for his state of mind).

Throughout the first two years of the war, Camus
did what all sensitive people, who were alertly following
what was going on in the world, were doing in those
days. He displayed an attitude of wait-and-see, evidently concerned with the clarification of many of the
theses he had put down in his previous publications. All
in all, he found little that needed revision and nothing
to retract. He wrote two additional very short essays, *Le
Minotaure ou la halte d'Oran* in 1939 and *Les Aman-
diers* in 1940. These showed no evidence of the shock-
ing experience of war that he was not to be spared later,

particularly during the time when he was involved in the resistance movement. He was still able to view and observe the events of the times from a distance, as it were, in a spirit of detachment, almost serenely.

In the course of the years 1940 and 1941, however, new and decisive perspectives opened up in Camus' creative work. He completed—without fanfare, almost as a matter of routine—two major works, neither of which, to be sure, was particularly impressive by its external magnitude, but both of which were to have a profound effect on Camus' contemporaries in terms of what we may call a clarification of awareness. Camus' first novel—or rather his first piece of book-length narrative prose—was completed in May 1940. This was *L'Etranger*. A philosophical essay on the absurd, *Le Mythe de Sisyphe*, followed in February 1941. These two works mark the beginning of a second period in Camus' creative career.

We cannot attach great importance to the question whether *L'Etranger* should be classed as a novel or as a narrative account. It is, in any event, a very significant prose work. The reader who sees its value primarily in the factual material it presents will tend to class the work as a narration. On the other hand, if we read the work without a clear reference to its time, regarding its hero primarily as the embodiment of a universally valid view of the condition of man, we shall evaluate it as a novel in the sense of the anti-novel and list it among the great monologues of man's spiritual situation that are a distinctive contribution of creative writing in the twentieth century.

Meursault, the hero of *L'Etranger,* is *homo persuasus,* that is, the man who consistently keeps faith with his truth and will not deny or betray it at any price. This makes him, in a sense, the antagonist incarnate of his time (1940). Meursault is an average person. His life is divided into work and diverting relaxation. He lives without firm commitments and knows responsibility and fidelity only to himself. He does his daily work mechanically. He complies with the rules of decency mechanically. He fulfills the commands of humanity minimally. He takes no interest in keen distinctions. He allows impressions and influences to come and affect him as they will. He is like a house without doors. He feels, but he never analyzes his feelings. Camus wrote:

"To me Meursault is not a human wreck but a man, bare and poor, who loves the sun that casts no shadows. He is by no means devoid of feeling, for the passion that imbues him, being profoundly stubborn, is a passion for the absolute and for truth. This truth is as yet negative. It is the truth of being and of feeling, but without it man's conquest of either himself or of the world would forever be impossible." [2]

Meursault's story is presented in the first person, implying that the reader is unwittingly drawn into a kind of partnership with the man. We are directly faced with his experiences and feel continuously impelled to wonder what we would do if we were in his place. This appears to have been Camus' precise objective. We first meet Meursault at his mother's deathbed. Together with a few women of the home for the aged near Algiers where his mother had died, Meursault is keeping the

death watch. He drinks coffee, smokes a cigarette,
dozes. There is no evidence of feeling, of inner involvement. He is present yet absent. He maintains this same
attitude during his mother's burial. He goes through the
motions which the situation calls for. The following
morning, back in Algiers—it is a Saturday—he meets
at the beach a young girl, Marie Cardona, whom he
once knew in a casual sort of way. That evening he takes
her to a movie, and she spends the night with him. The
following Sunday the two are the guests of a man
named Raymond, who lives on the same floor as Meursault. Raymond, who makes his living as a "protector"
of prostitutes, invites the two to spend the day with him
outside of Algiers at the place of a friend of his. There
they meet two Arabs who have been pursuing Raymond
for some time to avenge a girl of their race. Raymond
had unmercifully beaten this girl because he thought
that she had cheated him. There follows a free-for-all
among the men on the beach. Raymond is wounded. A
little while later Meursault happens to run into the two
Arabs again. In his pocket he still has the revolver that
Raymond had given him shortly before the fight.
Blinded and dazzled by the excess of sunlight, he shoots
down one of the Arabs and fires a few more bullets into
the dead body.

"Then I only felt the cymbals of the sun beating on
my forehead and saw in front of me the open blade of a
shining knife. It was a burning sword searing my lashes
and delving painfully into my eyes. That was the moment when everything lost its hold. The ocean exhaled a
fiery and dense breath that closed in upon me. It seemed

that the skies were opening up in all their expanse to inundate everything with a rain of fire. I grew tense all over, clenching the revolver in my hand. The trigger gave, I felt the smooth belly of the grip, and it was then —in the sharp and deafening snap of the report—that everything began. I tried to shake off the perspiration and the sun. I understood that I had destroyed the equilibrium of the day, the particular silence of the beach in which I had been happy. I fired four more times into the lifeless body which the bullets penetrated without leaving a trace. It was like four brief knocks on the door of unhappiness." [3]

Meursault is arrested and taken to jail. In the course of the trial, the prosecuting attorney makes the point that Meursault has in fact at all times been leading a disengaged and irresponsible life, verging on amorality. He is condemned to death. Meursault accepts the verdict, refusing all consolations of the Church because he does not believe in God, because he has known and has loved life on this earth and nothing beyond it. In fact, the thought of the absurdity of his death calms him.

" 'Well, I am going to die.' Sooner than others, to be sure. But everybody knows that life is not worth the trouble of living. Deep down I knew full well that it makes little difference whether a man dies at thirty or at sixty. After all, in both cases there are other men and women who go on living, for thousands of years. Nothing could be clearer, come to think of it. The one to die would always be me, now or twenty years from now. What bothered me a little, in the way I thought of it all at that moment, was the frightfully strong hold which the thought of another twenty years of life ahead of me seemed to have on my feelings. But I could get out of that by trying to imagine what my thoughts would be like twenty or so years from now, when I was bound to be in that same spot anyway. Once you know you have to die, how and when of course no longer matters." [4]

After this, Meursault has only one more wish:

"To round out everything, to make me feel less alone, I could only hope that on the day of my execution there would be a big crowd to watch me and that they would greet me with shouts of hate." [5]

It would be absolutely wrong to regard this final wish of Meursault's as blasphemy. Where there is no God, no god can be blasphemed. Where there has never been grace, Grace cannot suddenly appear. What Meursault asks for is no more than the confirmation of his fate in the form of a last consistent manifestation of hate by life itself, the senselessness of which he has come to recognize. He has never been really involved in anything. He has never been more than a blind tool in the arbitrary antics of this absurd life. He took no part in either the life or the death of his mother, none in the feelings of Marie, none in the death of the Arab who, in truth, was murdered by the sun and not by Meursault. Therefore he acknowledges guilt only because all those around him tell him that he is guilty: the prosecuting attorney, the court, the priest. In the end he actually comes to blows with the priest. It is only after the priest has left that he again feels free from evil.

What, then, was Camus' real message for his fellow men, the message which—from 1942 on, when the book was first presented to the public—he wished them to understand? Was this possibly a message that could be qualified as good tidings?

In the preface to the American edition of *L'Etranger,* written in 1955, Camus explained that Meursault was in fact condemned to death because "he does not play along. . . . In our society anyone who does not cry at the burial of his mother runs the risk of being condemned to death." [6] This may give us simultaneously a more direct understanding of the title of the book. Meursault is *l'étranger,* that is, "the stranger" or "the outsider" in a world standardized by the aesthetic conventions that men use to conceal from themselves and from others the ultimate impossibility of unraveling the riddle of life. They have invented pleasing rules of the game which make it easier for them to maintain an unperturbed balance even while they stand at the brink of the abyss. Yet in doing so they have also lost the urge to ask relentlessly the question of the meaning of life. Meursault, too, fails to ask that question. For him, the anonymous average man, all aspects of his demeanor were predetermined. There was nothing he had to do but accept the duties assigned to him. Thus it happens —and here lies the tragedy of his fate—that the occasion for his first experience of thought is provided by his first autonomous act, an act of violence, which simultaneously marks his end. But thought should precede the deed so that blind deeds may be prevented— blind deeds which are misdeeds in the truest sense of the word.

Camus, advocate of conscious awareness, looked

deeply into and through the suffering of the age which was his own. When *L'Etranger* appeared, Hitler and his henchmen ruled throughout virtually all of Europe. Autonomous thinking had more and more been ruled out, put out, extinguished. A central brain took care of thought for everyone. Meursault's fate perfectly exemplifies the fate of man who has been deprived of all vestiges of human dignity and who has been reduced to the passive existence of an animal. Meursault's fate stood out in sharp contour, in glaring colors against the bloody horizon of the age, even though the causes of his fate went farther back, to times long before the age of Hitler.

Those still able to see, the men and women whom the events of the day had neither blinded nor dazzled— and their numbers were, characteristically, larger in France than elsewhere in Europe, larger, in particular, than in Hitler's homeland—these men were ready to decipher the new presentation, the new interpretation, of the age. Beyond that they also recognized that a young writer had arisen in their midst whose prophetic acuity of vision, whose compressed powers of utterance backed the promise of further significant statements. It is quite remarkable to what extent Camus, starting from the time when *L'Etranger* was first published, appealed not only to the intellectuals and the fully matured but also, and in particular, to the working classes and to the young. With *L'Etranger* Camus' language had lost the last glimmer of smiling serenity which had imparted a certain poetic charm to his early essays. In its stead, perhaps evolved from it through an event of mutation, there was now a kind of grim and deathly humor, appropriate to the experiences in store—even in France during those years of war—for a man as incontrovertibly committed to justice as Camus. In an essay, *Prométhée aux enfers*, Camus conjured up these memories once again in 1946.

The year *L'Etranger* was first published—that is, 1942—was also the year of the publication of Camus' great philosophical essay on the absurd, *Le Mythe de Sisyphe*. It is, in a sense, a summary balance sheet of the store of concrete experiences of the first three decades of Camus' life. At the focal point of the entire discussion is the basic question of all philosophical endeavor: Is life worth the trouble it takes to live it? To avoid misunderstanding, let us state right here that Camus answers the question in the affirmative. But what is unusual in the book, what makes its reading a unique and critical experience, is the specific line of reasoning that leads the author to this affirmation. One would expect, after all, that a man who has recognized life to be meaningless, absurd, through and through irrational in its very essence cannot now have any concern but to dispose of life as rapidly as possible. To be fully consistent, this would seem to imply, he must commit suicide. Yet, it is hard to imagine a firmer rejection of suicide than that insisted upon by Camus. To him Sisyphus appeared to be the paradigm of the absurd life: Sisyphus the now proverbial hero of the ancient legend who was condemned, as punishment for his contempt of the gods, to roll uphill a rock which endlessly came rolling down again. By living as he must live, Sisyphus brings

the absurd to life. He knows the hopelessness of his relentless endeavor, which is the very essence of the punishment meted out to him. He knows it and despises it.
The absurd man is proud and therefore says Yes. Thus,
what was intended to debase and humiliate him is established by him as a world which is, a world in which he
alone can claim sovereignty.

"His fate is his. His rock is his own.[7] . . . This
universe which henceforth has no ruler is to him neither
sterile nor futile. Every grain in this boulder, every
flake of mineral in this night-pervaded mountain is to
him—to him alone—a world. Struggle as such, strug-
gling for the heights, is enough to fill a man's heart.
Sisyphus must be thought of as happy." [8]

The last sentence, "Sisyphus must be thought of as
happy," is the key to a full understanding of what
Camus' definition and interpretation of the absurd
means. That definition and interpretation—though Camus was in no way interested in earning a reputation as
a direct "benefactor of mankind"—must be of help to
men in an age of catastrophes in which life seems to
deny itself, as was the case during the years of the Second World War. Yet what really matters to Camus is the
underlying, ever-valid truth which an age of catastrophes will serve to make more palpably clear, to drive
home with more impressive evidence. "There is no fate
that cannot be overcome by contempt." [9] Meursault,
unwittingly, made this point, and Sisyphus, to repeat, is
a happy man.

Whoever imagines that there are ways out of the
absurd situation of life has fallen victim to the most

dreadful illusion imaginable. Philosophical systems and religions that point to possible solutions or, indeed, insist that we must accept their purported solutions were unacceptable to Camus, for his realm was entirely the realm of this world. Such systems were, to him, an integral component of the absurd itself.

"This world I can touch. I conclude from my touching it that it exists. That is the limit of what I know. The rest is theory.[10] . . . I shall forever remain a stranger to myself [11] . . . a stranger to myself and a stranger to the world." [12]

To Camus one of the distinctive traits of the absurd man is that he cannot believe in a hidden meaning of things, in a world of symbolic representation. The ultimate certainty which we possess is death. It denudes us, it extinguishes us. To rise up against death is hence our chief concern. Through such an uprising I give life a value. In a world of transient beauty—Camus accepted beauty as an essential basis of this world, in contrast to his great contemporary Jean-Paul Sartre, to whom that basis was "horror and the disgust resulting from it"— in a world of ephemeral beauty and absolute impassivity toward man's destiny, man therefore has the duty to take a stand against death with all the freedom of the mind that he can muster, with all the passion of his heart, for beyond death no realm of extraterrestrial hope is awaiting him.

"The point is that we must remain unreconciled to death, that we must not die willingly. Suicide is a misconception. The absurd man is bound to draw out all that can be drawn out, is bound to draw out himself.

The absurd is his ultimate tension, a tension which he maintains at all times through a unique effort, where he knows that it is in this awareness and in this uprising day in and day out that he bears witness to the only truth which is his, that he bears witness to the challenge. This is a first inference." [13]

Since life is devoid of significance, it follows that death too must be so. It further follows, to Camus' mind, that he who commits suicide disavows the absurd, for he acknowledges at least the possibility that death, by contrast to life, may have a meaning. Since, however, life is the only thing of which we can really be certain, the thought of a voluntary death must be rejected with the utmost rigor. Dignity and greatness are reserved for him who clings to life for as long as possible. Camus knew that to do so, to accept "clinging to life" as a principle, is not always easy, for the absurd often builds up around us, making us feel immured and threatening to choke us.

The focal point, the essence of all our encounters with the absurd and of our awareness of it, is—beyond a shadow of a doubt—the event of dying, that "blood-drenched mathematics which governs the constitution of our being." We may ask: Why? But this question leads us too easily to arrive at a compromise with death when the "denseness, the strangeness of the world," which are the core of the absurd, threaten to overwhelm us. It follows that we must accept the feeling of being immured which comes to us from what surrounds our lives, and yet we must remain faithful to life. The absurd man no longer knows the urge to break through the wall that surrounds him, for he no longer has the desire to leave time behind and partake of an eternity which does not exist. He adjusts himself as best he can to the impermeability of the wall which implies that it is forever his duty "to be in full," to become totally what he is. This is what matters.

According to Camus four human types fulfill this requirement the most completely and the most felicitously. They go through the history of mankind as prototypes of individuals who have what it takes to face the absurd proudly: Don Juan, the inveterate lover; the actor, spreading out over all the possibilities of life with utter unconcern of self-dissolution; the conqueror, who duplicates himself unendingly in the absolute deed; and the creative individual who embodies in his work most impressively the protest against the absurd life.

As the absurd man never takes leave of time—since to him there is no eternity—so Don Juan, whose concern is to be in touch with as many women as possible, evolves a richly intensified life in the here and now that overcomes the thought of death through pleasure. Don Juan establishes for himself an "ethics of quantity" that runs counter to every type of religious ethics. Conscious of the ephemerality of the many faces in this world whom he loves and intent on being ephemeral himself only in the form of loving which he has chosen, he knows himself to be magnanimous and free: Unceasingly he gives new life.

The actor, too, is forever a "giver of life": he "rules in a world of ephemerality." No man's fame is more fleeting than the actor's. But what makes for his greatness is his protean versatility, his refusal to be content with ever repeating the same form of life. To him the barrier has been removed between what a man strives to be and what in fact he is. What links the actor to the absurd man is that to him a premature death would be irreparable; nothing could compensate him for the faces and centuries through which he passes all his life long and which, to him, are this world, the only world, a world which crumbles in death. The Church knew why it regarded the actor as its most determined adversary.

The lust of the conqueror likewise derives from his fighting against death. His choice has been the deed, for he knows that deeds are done within time. He finds self-affirmation only in doing, if need be in doing vainly, even in defeat.

The true conqueror is no less aware of his ephemerality than are Don Juan and the actor. He, too, feels his full humanity only in spreading, in potentiating and in multiplying himself, and he knows that all this is revoked only, though of necessity, in death. That his deeds of conquest are not enough to improve men (or to cancel out the absurdity of life) is a knowledge he never doubts for even a moment's time, but the worth of those deeds lies precisely in the hopelessness of the protest which they embody. The conqueror's blows descend as lightning bolts and illuminate for a brief moment the wasteland of his life. He perishes with his body, and this knowledge is, to the conqueror, freedom. He has outtricked the absurd.

Finally, the creative individual is, to Camus, the permanent out-maneuverer of the absurd *par excellence*.

The greater he is the less he asks that his creations should last. He achieves self-fulfillment in the creative moment. While unceasingly enacting, in a potentiated form, the absurd itself, he manages in his own accounting to overcome it in an exemplary way. His life is a relentless protest against man's destiny.

Camus chose these four extreme types to illustrate how it is best possible to live with the fact of the absurd and, indeed, how this fact may at times impart to man a "royal power."

In the philosophy and the literature of our century —in which, throughout the lands of western civilization, nihilism in a multiplicity of forms has come to hold sway, has come, indeed, to be the dominant characteristic, so that positive points of reference and points of gravity are replaced by a "nihil" in many guises—the works of Camus represent a serious attempt to teach us how to transcend such nihilistic lessons and limits. We can learn from Camus to cling passionately to life— despite all the adversities we experience between birth and death, despite our awareness of the meaninglessness of life—to cling to it as to the only positive value existing in a form we can recognize. The moment we begin to rebel, to protest, against the absurd, against our role of subjects and victims of the absurd, in short, the moment we oppose our own will and our own acts to it or learn, like Sisyphus, to overcome our torment by contempt, we find ourselves incontestably in full possession of the life here and now that is ours, that is the only one we have. Seen thus, Camus' philosophy assumes the character of a new gospel of happiness.

Le Mythe de Sisyphe, completed in 1941, was published in 1943, the year which marked the turning point
in the war. Although the enslaved peoples of Europe
found new hope, they also realized that much blood
would flow before the day of their final liberation could
dawn. In times such as these, Camus' penetrating
awareness of the significance of the events—though
lurking behind them there seemed to be nothing but op-
pressive despair—remained, in spite of everything, a
manifestation of his "pessimism replete with hope."

On December 19, 1941, Gabriel Péri, a worker and
active member of the Communist resistance movement,
was executed by the army of occupation. Although
Camus' reaction to events during the first two years of
the war had been relatively aloof, this now gave way to
a strong and deep-felt indignation, especially since the
news reaching him from every side indicated that all
concept of a legal basis for government had been
annulled in the German-occupied countries and that
everywhere the terror of an all-powerful party dictator-
ship was running amok. In 1942 Camus took up contact
with the resistance group "Combat" and became a
member in 1943. The group circulated a newspaper,
also called *Combat*, typewritten at first but later in
mimeographed form, with the major objective of unmasking the political lies of the Vichy régime and the
German press agencies, in order to reduce the effective-
ness of Nazi propaganda. Information on arbitrary acts
of terror by locally established courts-martial, the mass
murder of Jews, and repressive measures against men
and women regarded as politically "unreliable" consti-

tuted a further aspect of *Combat*'s factual reporting. Camus assumed a more and more responsible role in directing the paper's editorial policy.

Through this work Camus met again his old friend Pascal Pia, the former editor-in-chief of *Alger Républicain*. He also met the writer André Malraux and the young poet René Leynaud. The latter was betrayed by collaborators, arrested on May 16, 1944, and executed shortly thereafter. Leynaud's death affected Camus more profoundly than any previous loss of a friend or a member of his family. When Leynaud's poems were published long after the end of the war, Camus supplied a deeply moving preface.

During this time Camus suffered another attack of tuberculosis. Under the circumstances it had seemed advisable for him and his wife not to stay together. In fact, the two were not to be reunited until after the war ended. Camus faced these vicissitudes with admirable energy and devoted himself, from a sense of urgently felt duty, to the underground newspaper. He was living in a village in the Auvergne, a part of France to which he never felt particularly attached. For reasons of safety and improved camouflage the editorial work was distributed over several places, and Camus had to keep going back and forth between Saint-Etienne and Lyons. As soon as conditions permitted, however, he was granted his wish to be sent to Paris. He arrived there around the end of 1943. In Paris he became a reader for the well-known publishing firm of Gallimard which previously had brought out *L'Etranger* and *Le Mythe de Sisyphe*. Camus held this position to the end of his life.

The nephew of his publisher—with whom he soon developed a deep friendship, in fact, a spiritual brotherhood—was the driver of the automobile in which the two, several years later, met their deaths.

Camus has left us no detailed account of his activity in the resistance movement. What brings us particularly close to Camus the resistance fighter, however, is four letters that were written in the course of the years 1943 and 1944 and published in 1945 under the title *Lettres à un ami allemand*. The publisher was Gallimard, who henceforth handled all of Camus' works. In these letters we find as nowhere else an "emotionally explosive" Camus, so passionately indignant at all the horrible wrong he was forced to witness that he seemed at times to be on the verge of turning into a nationalist. This can hardly be surprising if we consider that National-Socialist Germany under its charismatic leader (who long since had come to regard himself as the future ruler of the world) had the arrogance to claim that it was engaged in a messianic war for the redemption of mankind. Camus did not have the slightest tendency toward any kind of hubris (which is always fatal because it always involves the relinquishment of all desire for justice); yet here he could not help reacting with all the passion of his Mediterranean temperament. Yet even in his most scathing outbursts he never made the sweeping generalization that since the National Socialists were German, the Germans as a nation could be identified with the National Socialists.

The first and the second of these letters were written in July and December 1943 and published separately in two different periodicals in 1943 and 1944. The third

and fourth, written in April and July 1944, were not
published before the appearance of the whole series in
book form in 1945. There is some evidence that these
four pieces were based on conversations which two
young men, a German and a Frenchman, had had before the war and of which Camus had some knowledge.
Whether he himself was one of the partners in the conversation cannot be determined with certainty. There
also is no telling where these conversations may have
taken place. Camus himself was never in Germany and
never had a German friend. This suggests that the letters were addressed to an imaginary recipient. Bitter
resentment is their prevailing mood. "Hundreds of
thousands of men murdered at dawn, terrors of prison
walls, the soil of Europe steaming with corpses that
once were its children." [14] And yet—a point that cannot be overlooked, that cannot be overemphasized—
Camus did not avoid juxtaposing the words "German"
and "friend." He never abandoned the effort to be objective and never lost his sense of fairness and justice,
even in the extremity of an emotional outburst.

It was with some hesitation that Camus authorized
the republication of this book in later years and its dis-
semination in other countries. When the Italian edition
was being prepared, Camus took the occasion to write a
special preface which was taken over into all subsequent editions and translations of the work. A knowledge of this commentary is important, for it proves once
again to what extent Camus realized that clearness of
vision demands distance, particularly where statements
of documentary import are concerned.

"I cannot," Camus wrote, "allow these pages to ap-

pear once again in print without explaining what they
are. They were written and published clandestinely. It
was their purpose to carry a little light into the blind
struggle in which we were engaged at the time and thus
to make that struggle more effective. They are docu-
ments the composition of which was occasioned by circumstances, and this may well have resulted in their
failure to be just and fair on all counts. If I were asked
at this time to write about Germany after her defeat, I
would feel the need for writing in a somewhat different
vein. At any rate, I must try at least to prevent a misunderstanding. When the writer of these letters says 'you'
he does not mean 'you Germans' but 'you Nazis.' When
he says 'we,' he does not always mean 'we Frenchmen'
but 'we free Europeans.' It is not two nations that I
show in mutual opposition but two attitudes, even
though it may be true that at a particular moment in
history the two nations embodied the two mutually hostile attitudes. If I may use an expression which is not
my own, I love my country too much to be a nationalist.
And I know well, to take another view, that France and
Italy might well profit from opening up toward a
broader community. But that is a reckoning which fails
as yet to tally by a wide margin, and Europe is still torn.
I would, therefore, consider it shameful to give the impression that as a French author I could be hostile
toward a particular nation. What I do detest is hang-
men." [15]

The bitter truths contained in these four letters still
merit attention today. The letters still deserve to be
read, to be taken very seriously, to be thought through.

Above all, they should be placed in the hands of the young, for they provide far more than an apt basis for political discussions of certain aspects of the history of Franco-German relations; they are simultaneously a moving human document.

By August 24, 1944, thanks to the successful invasion of the Americans along the Atlantic coast, the war had practically come to an end as far as France was concerned, and the country thus had every chance to rise again from its ruins and its ashes. For Camus, too, the time had come for a new beginning; he was ready, to the limits of his resources, to help in the internal and external rebuilding of his country. He assumed, together with the inner circle of his tried and proven collaborators from the time of the resistance, the editorial responsibility for the newspaper *Combat* and held this position until 1947. He concentrated essentially on writing leading articles and was often the last to leave the editorial office of the paper, for on many days he also continued his work at Gallimard. He had meanwhile become a celebrity. This was the result no doubt of the publication of *L'Etranger* and *Le Mythe de Sisyphe*, but what inspired his following was still more the uncompromising loyalty to himself, the human greatness, with which he had held out for so many years in the resistance movement.

Jean-Paul Sartre, the leader of the existentialist school of philosophy, who was Camus' senior by eight years and whom Camus had met early in 1944 (a date marking the beginning of a friendship and collaboration which lasted until 1952), celebrated him as the "most versatile and richest," as the "last and most gifted heir of Chateaubriand." But Camus did not like the noisy, headline-conscious side of his calling and felt, in a sense, self-conscious when a critic or copy-writer extolled his merits a little too fulsomely. The poet in the writer Camus longed for quiet—particularly now that the furies of war had finally let go of his country. He had written his second stage play, *Le Malentendu,* which was published together with *Caligula* by Galli-mard in 1944 and which had its premiere at the Théâtre des Mathurins in the winter of that same year with Maria Casarès and Marcel Herrand in leading roles. *Le Malentendu* is strongly allegorical, and its success was hardly more than modest. Full recognition of Camus as a dramatist came only through *Caligula,* the premiere of which followed a short time later.

Altogether, the dramatist Camus was less success-ful than the novelist and essayist. The reason is not a lesser degree of intellectual acuity in his plays. No such lack characterizes them. What is true is that the dialogue makes the direct statement difficult and appears to be overburdened with implications of thought, so that the listener does not find it easy to follow the argument in all its phases. This holds particularly true for *Le Malen-tendu.* When we read this play, we cannot help feeling that it is the most poetic of all the works Camus wrote for the stage, but one cannot claim that speech and sit-uation always match perfectly.

The underlying fable had occupied Camus at least since the time when he wrote *L'Etranger*. In prison Meursault had found under his straw mattress a scrap of old newsprint with a story the beginning of which was missing.

"A man had left his village in Czechoslovakia to seek his fortune elsewhere. Twenty-five years later, now a rich man, he returned with his wife and a child. His mother and his sister were running an inn in his native village. In order to surprise them he arranged for his wife and child to stay at some other place and went alone to his mother, who did not recognize him when he arrived. As part of his little game he had the idea of renting a room, and in doing so he did not conceal his money. During the night his mother and his sister beat him to death with a hammer, robbed him, and threw his body into the river. The next morning his wife arrived. Unaware of what had happened, she revealed who the traveler was. The mother hanged herself. The sister threw herself into a well." [16]

This fable haunted Camus for years. In 1943 he sketched it out for the first time in dramatized form. (Camus liked to have several versions of a work at his disposal and to choose, before publication time, the one best suited to go into print.) The story, that is, its appeal to Camus, clearly belonged to a time which permitted the conception that the world, with its appearance of a guesthouse, is in fact a slaughterhouse. To be sure, the guiding principles of *Le Malentendu* could hardly be understood in psychological terms and still less on the basis of rational arguments. The French public was ill-prepared in 1945 to appreciate such multifaceted allegories and such philosophical implications in the absence of rational cogency and psychological realism. In a word, the play was felt to be lacking in logic. Its tragic tone, its refinement, its poetic presentation were no compensation to the audience which insisted—particularly in those days—on clarity of statement and precision of thought.

In his inner life, however, Camus at that time had moved ahead and beyond. The days of his youth were gone. Though the echoes of their remembrance lingered on, he had passed through the land of the foothills of knowledge, and he saw ahead new realms and new paths that were to take him to the summits of world fame.

4

~.~.~.~.~.~.~.~.~.~.~.~.~.~.~.~.~.~

Resistance

Peut-on être un saint sans Dieu, c'est le seul
problème concret que je connaisse aujourd'hui.[1]
[Can one, without God, be a saint? That is the only
concrete problem of which I am still aware.]

The life in the limelight of public attention which Camus was obliged to lead in Paris during the years after the liberation was at odds with the demands of his innermost being. Of course he was intelligent enough and also sufficiently adroit to hide this fact behind a mask of "coarse-grained crabbiness," but those close to him, the men and women he had taken into his confidence, could freely hear him admit how much he missed the atmosphere of the world that was properly his, a world far removed from all the vanity and all the ambition of a busy professional life. He was quite aware of all the deceit, all the lies that thrive luxuriantly wherever men live together in giant agglomerates, in the grim climate of a metropolis, where crime has its headquarters; and yet he sensed it to be his duty to persist and to go on living in this atmosphere at least for a while yet. What occupied his mind and filled his heart after the end of the holocaust of war was, above all, his concern with society, with the problems of rebuilding human communal life. He took it to be his most urgent duty to act among his contemporaries as a clearing agent, a catalyst of enlightenment, and wherever possible to extend his range of action beyond the frontiers of his country. It was in this spirit that he eagerly accepted an invitation to visit the United States, where he lectured at several American universities during the winter months of 1945–1946. He was jubilantly and enthusiastically received wherever he appeared, especially by the young. Camus liked traveling, especially alone, but this does not imply that his married life, which had been restored to its normal course in 1944, was anything less than happy. In 1945 he became the father of twins, Cathérine and Jean, who were to remain his only children.

Aside from his editorial work for *Combat* and his activity as a reader for Gallimard, his preoccupation with plans for new original works laid increasingly exacting claims on his time and energies. These original projects induced him in 1946 to give up his work for *Combat* for a while. Despite the numerous demands made on Camus by the political, cultural, and social life of the country and its capital in those days of passionate dedication to the task and the problems of national reconstruction, by 1947 he succeeded in completing his allegorical novel *La Peste,* which within a few years soared to unequalled pinnacles of world success and which doubtless belongs among the great European prose works of the middle of the century. From it future generations will be able to derive true and real knowledge of the suffering and also of the greatness of that era. With its abundance of allegorical figures, *La Peste,* a pandemonium of the epoch, came to be simultaneously a panhumanium, which was received enthusiastically by the press and the reading public, both being inclined to identify Camus with the central figure of his book, Doctor Rieux, and to celebrate the author as a "secular saint."

The chronicle of an epidemic of the plague within the walls of a town that is more and more cut off from the rest of the world and the search for ways and means to cope with it—that, in brief, is all that need be said about the external events recounted in this work which, again, is more concerned with fathoming the depth than with filling a broad canvas. As always in Camus, the thematic story is of modest circumference, and the elaboration of its thought content constitutes the real significance of the work. When Camus speaks, the essence of what he has to say can never be apprehended by asking "What?" but only by asking "How?"

The scene of the events of *La Peste* is Oran, the city in the desert, which Camus had already called, in *Le Minotaure*, "the dustiest of all cities," a place where "nothing stimulates the mind," where "even the ugly remains anonymous." As droves of rats surface one morning from their abodes in the sewer pipes, death begins to rule this plague-ridden city through them and with them. Since the people of Oran had always lived thoughtlessly, from day to day, the rule of terror has no trouble arrogating to itself the powers of the only tangible reality. It occupies the city, takes it over within the shortest spell of time, and dissolves all bonds that had previously sustained and unified the city. Three men, not more, are found who will accept the challenge and take up the fight against the deadly scourge with all their passion: the physician Dr. Rieux, his friend Tarrou, son of a state's attorney, and the journalist Rambert, who happens to be in town. Their joint struggle against the epidemic, their anxious awareness of their isolation from the rest of the world, the necessity to live their lives from moment to moment in the face of agony and death—all this arouses in them a sense of friendship and a clairvoyant courage they had never felt before, but which finally enables them to emerge victorious from their struggle against the plague. Evil is vanquished. The gates of the city open again, and the survivors again live for life's sake and for the sake of its joys. Yet the victors over evil know that they have not won an ultimate victory. They know that, once again, the dread hour can strike when—to men's misfortune and as a lesson to them—the plague will again awaken its rats to send them into an unprepared, happy town.

It is easy to see what outgrowths of his age Camus wanted the plague to suggest or symbolize: the man-eating catastrophes of the twentieth century, the concentration and annihilation camps, the technically sophisticated raids of individual Herostrati, and the wars. Camus began writing *La Peste* shortly after he had completed reading Daniel Defoe's *Journal of the Plague Year*, from which, quite fittingly, he took the motto for his own work: "It is as reasonable to represent one variety of imprisonment by another as it is to represent any really existing thing by one that does not exist." [2]

The two principal characters of the novel (whose voices and opinions strike us most personally as being Camus' own) are the physician Rieux and his friend Tarrou, who accompanies the doctor with the functions of a chronicler of the plague. It is only when the plague breaks out that Rieux begins in any way to recognize and understand himself and his innermost calling. It is the plague that guides him along the road to truth, and truth to him lies in taking up the struggle against the world as it now is, tormented by misery and pain, by injustice and violence, and governed by death. He does the humanly possible, yet does not in the least think of asking for recognition or applause. The strength he needs to persevere in his exacting daily work is constantly renewed (note once again Camus' leitmotiv) by his mother, who remains at all times in the background and would hardly have to be mentioned in a mere recounting of the action of the novel. The first victim lost by Rieux quite early in the book is his own wife. Thus freed from the last vestige of personal concern, he is now ready to pursue the more bitterly the struggle that demands his last ounce of strength. Surrounded day in and day out by events of horror that take place within his sight, he learns "there is more to admire in man than to despise." But even though he remains forever aware of the fated fact that all his efforts and all his endeavor cannot banish evil from this world, that "the bacillus of the plague" will never be eradicated, cannot be eradicated, these concessions are no reason for him to carry on his fight with less than supreme determination. By doing his part to alleviate the suffering of men, he creates, of himself and within himself, a force that opposes the senselessness of life (and of suffering), and he is therefore able to win out over the plague and over death. Nothing else matters to him. In his motivation, once again, no share falls to emotionally charitable elements.

Tarrou's case is quite different. He feels morally infected by his father, the state's attorney, whom he regards as in reality a recruiting officer in the employ of death. Tarrou had left home one day after he had been present when a death sentence was proclaimed and, somewhat later, when a man condemned to death was executed. Out of that experience grew his militant determination to oppose death and killing everywhere and at all times. He is convinced that nothing in the world can justify a death sentence. He places himself at the head of a corps of volunteers in the struggle against the plague and ultimately, in full acceptance of this consequence, loses his life. Perhaps he has thus become "a saint without God."

Rambert, the third member of the trio, happens to be in Oran on an assignment for his newspaper when the epidemic breaks out. At first he tries to escape the horror and the threat to his person, mainly in order to rejoin the woman he loves. However, his decision to leave is reached too late, and he has to stay on. He now works alongside Rieux until the epidemic is over, and the city finally releases him. He emerges from all the suffering a man of greater maturity.

And then there is the great antagonist, the Jesuit father Paneloux, who tries to teach the population to interpret this scourge of God as a just punishment for their sins and who brings them the solace of the Church. "My brethren, you are in distress. My brethren, you deserve it." [3]

It is his sense of Christian duty that induces him to join the fight against the epidemic, but after a while he cannot prevent the catastrophic conditions from plunging him into a state of somber dejection. Bent by the weight of what he has had to live through, he accepts God's will without a murmur, resigned to death in solitude. Yet, in reality, he remains passive as he faces the suffering of men. Rieux feels at most a detached respect for him, but neither understanding nor sympathy.

The somber panorama of a city wasting away under the castigations of the plague is again a wonderfully clear parable to communicate Camus' mature knowledge and his message a few short years after the end of the most trying ordeal for all mankind, the Second World War. The plague embodies the negation of every last breath of life on earth; it embodies all that instigates or condones murder and execution. It embodies not only wars but every bureaucratic excess, every excessive automation and automatization that uses humans and in the process forgets their humanity, that conjures up the danger of "maiming" humans—to cite a concept which occurs time and again in Camus' appeals to men's reason and sense of responsibility. Let us read what Camus himself wrote (as early as December 1942) in one of his notebooks:

"I propose to express through the plague the sense of suffocation which all of us have experienced and the atmosphere of threat and exile in which all of us have lived. I propose at the same time to extend this interpretation to the concept of existence in general. The plague will trace the picture of those who during this war have had as their lot reflection, silence—and moral suffering." [4]

This statement makes quite clear that Camus did not want *La Peste* to be understood exclusively in terms of its allusions to the current happenings in history. To be sure, these had been the immediate incentive to write the book, but Camus reached out far beyond the time-bound occasion to reveal once again, by means of a hypertransparent illustration, the absurdity of man's life situation in general. We recall the epistemological essence of *Le Mythe de Sisyphe* and the ethical imperative it implied for the human individual, and we find that it is as an embodiment of both that Camus developed the figure of Dr. Rieux, who indeed succeeded in having others emulate his example.

Time and again the question has been raised whether—subconsciously perhaps—Camus introduced in *La Peste*, in the person of his Dr. Rieux, a protagonist of Christian ideals and Christian love of neighbor. Christian theologians, in particular—naturally and urgently intent on "saving" for their message a man as uncompromising in his ethical postulates as Camus doubtless was—have, time and again, endeavored to have that question answered in their favor. I am convinced, however, that the question is to be answered in the negative. Camus spoke of himself—as does Tarrou —as an atheist. The good which he himself did and which he had his characters do was always the expression of a consciously rational attitude, never that of the individual's awareness of being, through grace, among the chosen in the sense of a divine revelation. The ethical grandeur of *La Peste* can be understood only in terms of an atheistic manifesto. The work is an expression of the author's respect for all life. In full knowledge of the ephemerality of everything living, Camus strove to help preserve life—human life—for as long as possible, in as unperturbed a form as possible, for Camus knew—and this imparts both strength and direction to his endeavor—that life is man's only possession and that he possesses it only once. This is the ultimate moral principle which Camus has to teach. And Camus was a great moralist, one of the greatest of our century. But it is a profound misevaluation to suggest that the coincidence of renunciation and dedication in his concept of morality bears witness to a religious bent. There is no need to qualify in any way the assertion that Camus' views are expressed in Rieux's remarks to Paneloux:

"The salvation of man—that is too big a word for me. I cannot go that far. It is man's well-being that interests me—his well-being, first of all. . . .[5]

"At present there are people who are sick, and the sick need to be healed. When that is done, they may begin to think and so may I. What is most urgent now is to heal them. I fight for them as best I can, that is all. . . .[6]

"Since the rules of the world are managed by death, it is perhaps best for God, too, that we do not believe in Him and fight instead with all our strength against death without lifting our eyes to the heavens from where He does not speak." [7]

The year of publication of *La Peste* was also the year when Camus gave up his editorial position with *Le Combat* for good. He ceded his place to Claude Bourdet, to whom he had been linked by close bonds of friendship since the earliest days of his work in the resistance movement. More and more Camus withdrew, quite generally, from all journalistic work. He intervened in the arena of clashing political opinions only when truly momentous questions were involved, such as the Algerian crisis, the uprising in East Berlin, or the revolt in Hungary. A point apart remained his feeling of attachment, of innermost affinity, to Algeria—the land and the destinies of its people. These bonds grew stronger as time went on. Mature now on many levels, Camus kept reverting to Algerian themes.

His passion for the theater, too, continued unabated. While he was still at work on the manuscript of *La Peste*, he began giving thought to the plan of dramatizing a closely related theme, and when Jean-Louis Barrault—even in those days one of the most promising young actors and stage directors of postwar France—approached him with the suggestion to work out a stage version of Daniel Defoe's *Journal of the Plague Year* (which Barrault, too, had just finished reading), Camus had no reason to hesitate. In 1948 Camus' new play, *L'Etat de siège*, had its premiere at the Théâtre Marigny with Barrault and his wife Madeleine Renaud and with Maria Casarès and Pierre Brasseur in the cast. The background music was written by Arthur Honegger.

In a preface to *L'Etat de siège*, written by Camus in November 1948, he stated explicitly that he followed Barrault's suggestion only to the extent that he omitted all references and allusions to Defoe's diary. What he was after was rather a myth which the public of 1948 would be able to grasp without laborious explanations. At the same time he could not have been satisfied with merely transposing his novel *La Peste* into a stage version. As Barrault conceived of it, the play was to be "total theater," that is, it was "to strive explicitly to use all expressive forms of the stage, the lyrical monologue as well as collective acting, pantomime, conventional dialogue, farce, and chorus."

In the skies over a city in Spain—Cadiz—a comet appears to announce a baleful occurrence to the population and its governor. Soon thereafter two personages appear, both in uniform, the one a somewhat voluminous male, the other his secretary. The man in uniform is the plague, his female companion and secretary is death. They proclaim that the city is in a state of siege, and the governor gives in to their suggestive power. The plague establishes a totalitarian regime of terror. It finds a henchman in Nada, an amoral drunkard, who soon advances to the rank of an official of the new regime, in which capacity he proceeds to prepare rigged elections. To Nada's great satisfaction, the citizens begin to be afraid of one another, with no one feeling certain that his next of kin is not an informer. Two young lovers are the only ones to rebel against the new totalitarian regime, the student Diego and the girl Victoria. The "secretary," seeing that Diego has broken through a barricade of fear, that he has overcome fear, is forced to admit that she is powerless against him. His example finds emulators. The power of the "plague" is more and more undermined. Now the plague, in order to assure the undisturbed continuation of its own rule, offers Diego a chance to escape together with Victoria. Diego refuses. Then the "secretary" (death) takes Diego away while returning Victoria to life. This signifies that Victoria buys back the freedom of the city at the expense of sacrificing the man she loves. When the plague and death move on, the state of siege is lifted, freedom can return.

We see another allegorical play, a moral lesson of
the need for courage which alone enables human beings
to meet and to cope with the inhuman. In its overall
mood, the play is reminiscent of the "moralities" that
were so popular toward the end of the Middle Ages and
which are now regarded as an early form of the theater
"as a moral institution." Yet, once again, despite the
lucid honesty and the passionate intensity of his inten-
tion, Camus did not really succeed in making the
finished product fully balanced or commensurate with
the idea he had conceived. Although the coming to
power of the plague is deeply convincing, nothing of the
sort could be said about the forces representing the op-
posite pole. The figures of the two lovers remain unmo-
tivated and have the feel of paper. The second half of
the work is no longer under the control of the dramatist
and appears instead to be a manifesto or a plea. The
play as a whole lacks continuity. It is not difficult to
understand that *L'Etat de siège* had to fall flat with both
the press and the public.

Camus achieved a correspondingly greater stage
success one year later, on December 15, 1949, when his
drama *Les Justes* opened—as *Caligula* had in 1945—
with Maria Casarès as the leading actress, and again—
like the eminently successful *Caligula*—at the Théâtre
Hébertot in Paris.

In this play Camus presented a historical subject:
the activities of a small fighting unit of Russian terrorists who carried out a series of bombing raids in 1905.
Camus was stimulated to handle this subject for the
stage by the memoirs of the Russian terrorist Boris
Savinkov (*Souvenirs d'un terroriste* [Memoirs of a ter-

rorist] Paris, 1931), in which the justification of political murder appears to be the writer's major concern. In
Camus' play we are introduced to five terrorists, one of
whom, Kaliayev, is chosen to throw a bomb on February 2, 1905, into the carriage taking the Grand Duke
to the theater. But during the split second that it takes
the carriage to pass by Kaliayev, he sees that against all
expectations two children, the Duke's nephew and
niece, are seated inside, and this is enough to paralyze
the would-be assassin's hand. He is unable to murder
innocent children. He wanted to blast tyranny, but he
had never thought of the deed as being an act of blind
fury. When he undertakes to justify his behavior to his
comrades, they all endorse his contention that innocent
children must not be killed. The only exception is
Stepan Fyodorov, who has learned in the hardest
school, the penal colony, to dispense with such nice distinctions. However, the attempt on the Grand Duke's
life has only been postponed. It is carried out two days
later. Kaliayev is apprehended and imprisoned. He rejects every form of clemency. A visit from the Grand
Duchess, who forgives him in a Christian spirit, cannot
change his attitude. He continues to insist that he must
be condemned to death. He cannot feel that he is one of
the just unless he is ready to pay with his own life for
the murder he has committed. The solace offered him
by the Church he likewise rejects, for he knows of another that, to him, is better: the love of Dora Dulyebov,
a revolutionary who shares his views. Thus his profession of faith in life attains fulfillment in a tragic climax.
Dora avows in the presence of Kaliayev's comrades,

whom he refuses to betray at any price, that she will be the one to throw the next bomb. Now Stepan, too, cannot help admiring Kaliayev's attitude.

In this ultimate consistency, that of the revolutionary who kills and atones—not in contrite repentance but only in order to restore the integrity of justice—Camus momentarily reached the epic dimensions of the problem of guilt and expiation that are found in ancient Greek tragedy. In particular, the spiritual vitality he succeeded in imparting to the fourth act may account for the raving acclaim that was accorded him after the premiere of the play. He had not changed the content of Savinkov's sober account, but had raised it to the level of meaningful poetry, to produce what is doubtless his most powerful and—through its inner appeal—most effective drama.

During the summer of 1949 Camus had accepted an invitation of the government to visit South America, where his mission included the presentation of public lectures. Soon after his return a recurrence of his illness forced him once again to hold back and husband his resources. He withdrew from public life to a greater extent than ever before and produced, in quantitative terms, very little in the course of the ensuing two years. The total fruit of this solitude was *L'Homme révolté*, the final revision of which he carried out during the years from 1949 to 1951, with the major portion of the work given over to abstract discussions. It represents essentially an attempt to find a satisfactory answer to the one question which had been left pending in *Le Mythe de Sisyphe*, that is, the question whether it is possible "within the confines of nihilism itself to find the means for its liquidation." Camus himself modestly called his essay another "effort to understand our time."

The theme of the work had first been among Camus' preoccupations as early as the days of *Le Mythe de Sisyphe,* which he kept meaning to continue. In his relentless endeavor to discover beyond the social and hence external distress of modern man, the ultimate bases of man's metaphysical distress, he had arrived at his own version of the nihilistic tenets which meanwhile came to hold sway everywhere in the most varied forms and under the most different masks. In *L'Homme ré-volté* it now was Camus' objective to clarify the premises that had led to the predominance of nihilism virtually in all parts of the western world. The work thus represents a critical review of the revolutions of the last two centuries and of the philosophies and literatures that influenced them. Since nihilism is an attitude or state of mind, Camus confronted it with the instrumentalities of the intellect.

As always, he started out from the individual human being.

"What is a man in revolt? A man who says no. But his refusal is not a renunciation. He is also a man who says yes, beginning with his very first move." [8]

But the man who says no, by opposing his will to that of another, achieves awareness of himself in a stronger form. "I revolt, therefore I am." Since this revolt results all too often from the vicarious experience of the oppression suffered by others, Camus is immediately able to take the next step: "I revolt, therefore we are." [9] And once again, from the first page of the book, Camus' basic attitude is apparent—a sense of solidarity with his fellow men, which he never abandoned either as a creative writer or as an abstract thinker.

In the figure of Prometheus Camus saw the model and prototype of all those in metaphysical revolt, but Prometheus too, in the course of the centuries, underwent an evolution which in the end reduced man's revolt to forms and norms, regulating it, packaging it in ideologies, and allowing it finally to degenerate and be petrified in totalitarian forms of social organization which are "the winter of the world" in which we now live.

"And so Prometheus pursues his astounding itinerary. Proclaiming his hatred of the gods and his love of man, he turns away with contempt from Zeus and goes to mingle with mortal men whom he leads in their assault on the heavens. But men are weak. Men are cowardly. They need to be organized. They seek the pleasures and the happiness of the moment. They must be taught to refuse, for the sake of their growth, the sweetnesses of the present. So Prometheus, too, becomes a taskmaster who starts out teaching and winds up commanding. The struggle drags on and proves exhausting. The men lose faith in their ability to reach the City of Light; they are no longer certain that it exists. They need to be saved from themselves. The leader assures them that he knows the city, that he alone knows it. The doubters shall be banished to the desert, chained to a rock, abandoned for the birds of prey to feed on. The others march on in darkness, following the leader who ponders and strides on alone. Prometheus in his solitude has become a god ruling over men in their solitude. But from his conquest of Zeus he only retains the solitude and the cruelty of Zeus. He is no longer Prometheus; he is Caesar. The real, the eternal Prometheus has taken on the appearance of one of his victims. The same call, the same scream, surging from the depth of ages, echoes on and on deep in the desert of Cimmeria." [10]

It is not difficult to reduce to a single formula what Camus meant to express through this timely variation of the myth of Prometheus. The revolt of men, which is an expression of their search for justice—a natural reaction to the absurdity of their situation in life—has been betrayed in the realm of realities by the revolutions of peoples. It is for this reason that we must draw a concise line of differentiation between the concepts of "revolt" and "revolution." In the time of "unholiness" in which we live, revolt has become the expression of our reality, indeed of our dignity. Throughout history revolutions have utilized the revolts of men, pursuing through these revolts their own egotistic goals, which they attained in the end with disastrous consequences for all.

Using as an example the great "ideologists," such as Sade, Hegel, Marx, Nietzsche, and others, Camus showed that their historical trail-blazing led to the establishment of states based—rationally or irrationally —on terror. From the terror of the individual in revolt the terror of the state emerged, the terror of organized masses which accepts and uses mass murder as a means sanctified by the objectives it is made to serve. Whether, as in fascism, man takes on the role of god or whether, as in bolshevism, reason as the wielder of Marxist dialectics has usurped the role of leadership in the state, in either case the underlying tragedy is the betrayal of the revolt of the individual. Surely at the beginning of the great revolutions men of outstanding qualifications did assume positions of leadership but, regardless of the honest ethical fervor that inspired them, the moment their individual revolts suffered contamination and corruption at the hands of doctrinaires and functionaries and were pressed into the service of egotistic interests, they could only wreak harm to the community of men. Therefore we cannot achieve a full and fair appraisal of the dilemma of man when we attempt to interpret it exclusively in historical terms. Throughout the nineteenth century the prevailing historicistic trend tended to elevate history itself to the rank of an almighty goddess against whose inexorably predetermined course no successful revolt was possible; and since men accepted this dogma on faith, they deluded themselves, enclosed themselves in fortress walls, and a perspective of a "better future" remained confined in their experience within the narrow frame of loopholes in these massive walls. But the only result that Camus considered sensible and justified has the distinctive characteristics that it can be the concern of each and every man and that it runs counter to all usurped power. The revolt of the individual entails at all times a restraining component in its positive orientation, a certain sense of "measure," which revolutions discard. So Camus had to veer away

from the historicistic patterns of thought which, implying ultimate justification of everything and anything,
have come to be, by virtue of a corroding habit, a
matter of day-to-day routine for us. Explicitly and
solemnly he rejected their unnatural tyrannical rule of
men. To what extent he had faith that man could overcome this condition is clearly apparent in the following
quotation from *L'Homme révolté*:

"When then the revolution, in the name of power
and of history, has become a restraintless and murder-
ous system, a new revolt is ready to be consecrated in
the name of restraint and of life. This is the point we
have reached. After this night another dawn must come
of which we already are vaguely aware. We need but
fight for it, and it shall be. We all, amidst ruins, prepare
beyond our nihilism for a rebirth. Few, however, know
it." [11]

But Camus was above all an artist. Thus it would
have been impossible for him to respond to the catastrophic world situation of our century except through
an ideal born of the union of aesthetically detached
serenity with philosophically exacting rigor, that is,
specifically, the ideal of a new definition of the relations
of give and take between the individual and the group
of which the individual is an integral part. With bolshevism as an example, Camus showed how these relations,
having undergone total dehumanization, were practically annulled.

"The Russian concentration-camp state did accomplish the dialectical transition from the government
of men to the administration of things by treating men
as things." [12]

Camus referred to the darkness descending upon mankind through this abortive development of revolutions as the blight of "midnight thought" and opposed to it the powers of "meridional thought" (*la pensée du midi*). He discussed its greatness at length, presented examples of its realization, and explained that its contribution could help revolutions to establish new civilizations instead of being perverted to terror and tyranny.

Since Camus thought of himself as an heir to "Mediterranean" traditions, it is not surprising that he persisted in upholding in this twentieth century a type of social morality in which we discern essential elements of an aristocratic character. Thus he demands that the individual develop to the fullest in keeping with aesthetic axioms while heeding to the same extent the ethical demands for the individual's integration in a greater communal whole. In this moderation, in this self-restraint as the ancients taught it for the sake of norms and standards in the individual's inclinations and interests, Camus recognized one of the timeless truths in world history. (It is only fair to state that he idealized antiquity and that he failed to note in this connection that Mediterranean countries such as Italy and Spain, too, had proved capable of generating totalitarian regimes.)

In the last analysis, Camus' primary concern was at all times the happiness of man, and this, as he saw it, was threatened above all by the excesses, the lack of restraint, of individuals. His own attitude, exemplified again and again, was one of brotherliness, of considerateness, of paying heed to his companions, and this gave him the right to proclaim the revolt of the indi-

vidual as his basic value, as the most natural and most
creative necessity of life itself. For "in the revolt conscience awakens."

The reception of the book by the public is one of
the *causes célèbres* in the annals of modern literary history. The dissent it aroused was in part riotous in intensity. The battle of words, which lasted for more than
one year, was waged, particularly by the opposition,
with all the devices of aggressive polemics. Its principal
organ was the periodical *Les Temps Modernes*, edited
by Jean-Paul Sartre, Camus' old friend and brother in
arms during the days of the resistance movement. In
August 1952 the friendship of the two men came to an
end. In a disputation which filled some eighty pages in
print, Sartre reproached Camus with having betrayed
Communism and, in particular, with having become
guilty of a cowardly return to transcendental thought. It
is surely what we have called the Mediterranean idea of
Camus that impressed Sartre in this sense, for Sartre,
the autonomous creator of his own freedom, could
neither accept nor tolerate any kind of extraneous obligation. In the opinion of the defenders of the book, on
the other hand, it marked in Camus' development the
beginning of a new stage of maturity whose distinctive
characteristic was no longer an *engagement* in terms of
a specific dialectical dogma and orientation but a more
comprehensive, more inclusive participation in life as
such. To this Camus was to erect additional convincing
and impressively beautiful monuments during the remaining seven years of his creative life.

In November 1952 Camus broke with UNESCO,

which had admitted Franco's Spain to membership. In this we can only see further evidence of the uncompromising rigor which determined Camus' personal attitude in all things. If the hair-splitting philosophical schoolmaster discovers in Camus' extrapersonal thought an occasional contradiction of pure logic, this can only serve to lend greater credence to the poet in him who was indeed at times overshadowed by the thinker. Camus' life was filled with a sense of justice which at all times made him stand up for principles. There is probably no better proof of this than the sharp reply Camus addressed in 1948 to the Christian existentialist Gabriel Marcel, who felt he could defend Franco's Spain while condemning Russia because the political victims of Russian Communism exceeded in numbers those claimed by the Spanish Civil War.

After the publication of *L'Homme révolté*, the defense of which had cost Camus much energy, he seems to have experienced a certain lassitude that did not allow him to progress in new works beyond the planning stage. In 1954, in fact, he wrote nothing at all. It is also possible that all the animosity stirred up by the publication of *L'Homme révolté* renewed his longing for a world of greater "innocence." In any event, in 1953 Camus turned once more with all his strength to his old love, the stage. An accidental turn of events provided the occasion; he was called upon to take over the direction of the summer theater at Angers (in the Maine-et-Loire) as a substitute for his friend Marcel Herrand, who had fallen ill. Full of enthusiasm about the possibilities of the open-air stage in an old castle courtyard, he participated in these festivals in subsequent summers as well. With *La Devoción de la cruz* by Calderón and *Les Esprits* by Larivey (a sixteenth-century French dramatist of Italian descent), both of which Camus had revised for the modern stage—the former under the title of *La Dévotion à la croix*—he introduced himself, many years after his Algerian beginnings in the field, as a craftsman of the stage, also in metropolitan France, both as an adapter of plays and as the director of their performances. In neither respect was Camus a radical advocate of reform for the sake of reform. He was no fanatic of sobriety or of alienation of the kind represented at about the same time in Germany by Bertold Brecht. Rather, he granted the theater the theater's due, especially in matters of décor and display and thus revealed his close kinship with the theater of Barrault. In any event, he was a director who knew in full conceptual clarity what he wanted and also how to impart to his actors a congenial awareness of his objectives. In addition, he proved himself in the theater, as he had done so often elsewhere in the course of his life, an ideal leader of men, being able to play in any group venture the role of a *primus inter pares.* The great success which he achieved with his stagings in the provinces gave him the opportunity in 1956 to participate actively and creatively in the theatrical life of Paris.

And so it came to pass that it was in Paris that Camus achieved his greatest stage success. His adaptation of William Faulkner's *Requiem for a Nun* (under the title of *Requiem pour une nonne*), ran for fully two years at the Théâtre des Mathurins, for a while with

Camus in the principal male role, before a sold-out house. It is the story of a Negress who is found guilty of murder and who makes an extraordinary atonement as an adult woman for the foolhardy adventures of her youth. The phases through which the tragedy pursues its course—the court of law, an office, the prison—serve Camus once again as backdrops for his real objective, the demonstration of the incongruity of jurisdiction and penal practice to the deeper realities of human guilt.

It would seem that Camus had a luckier hand in his stage adaptations than in his original plays. Apart from the works from world literature already mentioned, he arranged for the modern French theater *Caballero de Olmedo* by the Spaniard Lope de Vega (*Le Chevalier d'Olmedo*), *Un Caso clinico* by the contemporary Italian Dino Buzzati (born 1906), which he rendered as *Un Cas intéressant*, and Dostoevski's *The Demons*, with the French title *Les Possédés*. All these works, without a single exception, were very successful. Camus' plan for an original play, *Don Juan*, was never carried out.

Throughout his entire life Camus felt a particular affinity for Dostoevski's work. It was a risky undertaking, bordering on the impossible, to reduce the Russian novelist's sprawling epic to a play of normal duration. The procedure chosen by Camus was virtually the only one possible, consisting in selecting a few episodes from the novel. In combining them Camus displayed exceptional dramaturgic skill, for despite the fact that his finished product ran through twenty-two separate scenes, there is no break in the dramatic continuity, no lagging in dramatic interest. By introducing a narrator with the function of providing commentaries before and after the individual scenes, Camus succeeded in condensing the indispensable nondramatic elements of the action to such an extent that the spectator has the impression of a perfect unity of action, which results in turn in a more compressed and hence more impressive presentation of Dostoevski's ideas. Ever since his adolescence, Camus had counted Dostoevski among the great prophets of world literature, standing side by side with Homer, Cervantes, and Shakespeare. He saw in Dostoevski the desperate proclaimer of occidental nihilism. But whereas the Russian genius, having imbued virtually all his characters with a spirit of human hopelessness, in the end oriented his persistent quest for hope toward the concept of God, Camus replaced this ultimate transcendentalism by his reliance on man. The topics of suicide and revolt, discussed in Dostoevski's novel *The Demons* in lengthy conversations replete with fantastic visions of future human happiness and social reform, all centering in vastly expanded circles on the problem of freedom, afforded Camus once again an opportunity to speak from the depth of his knowledge of men and the problems confronting them in our day and age.

"The characters created by Dostoevski, we now fully realize, are neither strange nor absurd. They resemble us. We have hearts like theirs. And if this book, *The Demons*, is a prophetic book, this is so not simply because it announces our nihilism but also because it presents torn or dead souls that are incapable of love while suffering for this lack, that want to believe but cannot, precisely those that make up our societies today, that haunt our world of the spirit." [13]

The first performance of this work, Camus' last for the stage, took place in January 1959 at the Théâtre Antoine in Paris. The following winter the Herbert Company toured the country with this play which suitably crowned and prematurely concluded Camus' career as a craftsman and creator of the stage.

He was to attain his ultimate maturity, however, in the field of narrative prose.

5

~.~.~.~.~.~.~.~.~.~.~.~.~.~.~.~.~.~.~.~

Light Regained

*Au milieu de l'hiver j'apprenais enfin
qu'il y avait en moi un été invincible.*[1]
[In the middle of winter I understood at last
that there is in me an invincible summer.]

We have broken the chronological continuity of our presentation of Camus' career in order to continue uninterrupted our presentation of Camus' work as a playwright and adapter for the stage. Yet the years following the publication of *L'Homme révolté* (1952–1959), were marked not only by Camus' increased theater activity but also—apart from a few journalistic contributions dealing with political events of the day—by several prose works which, though short, are crucially important because of their content.

We have mentioned before that Camus' early works *L'Envers et l'endroit* and *Noces* were republished in 1954. However, this treasury of Camus' essays was now enriched, not only by an informative introduction but also by a number of additional newer pieces (incorporated in the collection *L'Eté*) that rank among Camus' most beautiful prose compositions. We refer to the three essays, *L'Enigme* (1950), *Retour à Tipasa* (1952), and *La Mer au plus près* (1953). As the titles suggest, here Camus returned, on a higher plane of consciousness, as it were, to his sources. That he was quite aware of this return, which was tantamount to a rediscovery of his own self and of his artistic call, is clearly apparent from the text, written sometime between 1951 and 1954, of the new edition of *L'Envers et l'endroit*.

"Indeed, there is nothing to prevent me from dreaming, in this hour of exile, for I do know at least this, know it through certain knowledge, that the work of a man's life is nothing other than a meandering quest to find again, through the detours of art, the two or three simple and great images upon which the heart, at the very first, opened up." [2]

We know precisely what these images, never concealed and never dimmed, were in Albert Camus' life.

"All that bears witness to truth, as I see it: this old woman, a mother who speaks but rarely, light on the olive trees of Italy, love that is lonely at times and a world filled, at other times, with people." [3]

The three prose pieces with which we are concerned here—though certainly not representative, in classical precision, of the literary genre of the essay—are proof that Camus had definitively won out over despair. However significant, however creative the role of despair may have been in his life, however courageously he had ventured forth in all directions to the ultimate confines of its realm, he did not, in the end, persist in clinging to it but outgrew it, grew out of its limits and beyond them. It came to be the basis on which he achieved a breakthrough to a new light, and this light, indeed, he felt to be a natural continuation of despair. And although it may seem for a moment as though the term "light" were used here in a metaphoric sense, yet —after all is said and done—the light we speak of came in the end to be identified with precisely the light under which and in which he had grown up.

"In the blackest hours of our nihilism I sought to find reasons to go beyond this nihilism. I did so certainly not out of virtue and certainly not out of a rare transfiguration but out of an instinctive loyalty to the light in which I was born, a light through which, for thousands of years, men have learned to salute, to welcome life even when it meant suffering. . . . From the core of our work, bleak though it be, radiates an inexhaustible sun, the same that cries out today over the plains and hills." [4]

The despair had come to be an "enigma," one might feel tempted to say a "miracle," if it were not for the fact that this term—quite contrary to Camus' intentions—would lead too easily to erroneous associations.

This very same experience—this same lived experience—pervades Camus' *Retour à Tipasa*. Here the "exile" Camus returns to his unlost realm of beauty. "To live a second time we need grace, forgetfulness of our self, or a land in which we are at home." [5] Camus once again walks through Algiers, once again starts out on the road to Tipasa, and at last in fact reaches the Chenoua mountain, the "old moss-covered god whom nothing can shake, refuge and port to his sons, of whom I am one." [6] But before he succumbs to the powerful murmur of his ever-flowing sources—and lest he stay there and make his return permanent—a sense of duty reminds him of the world of cities "built of stone and vapors" [7] which have just claims on him, a sense of duty toward his family.

"But perhaps some day, when we are ready to die of exhaustion and of ignorance, I shall be able to renounce our shrieking tombs to go and lie down in the valley, under the same light, and learn for the last time that which I know." [8]

A romantic Camus such as we have not met before with the same intensity of feeling, but we find him once again at a still higher level of intensity in *La Mer au plus près*. This was to be the last of his essays and as such may almost be called a profession of faith. Camus himself called it "a shipboard diary," and we may assume that its utterances hark back to experiences which Camus had during his sea voyage to South America. But these, insofar as they did play a role, represented—as was generally the case in Camus' works—no more than starting points for objective crystallizations. In its external form, *La Mer au plus près* is the most loosely knit of all Camus' essays. It is a series of aphoristic observations, at times with a pronouncedly lyrical, and at times with a more strictly intellectual, orientation. The closing aphorism is the one most clearly indicative of the new perspectives under which Camus was henceforth to pursue his course.

"I have always had the feeling that I lived on the high seas, imperiled, at the core of a royal happiness." [9]

In May 1955, Camus' old dream of a trip to Greece finally came true. It did not result in a literary precipitate, which is quite surprising, for Camus had always found it impossible to refrain from responding directly to any kind of direct stimulus. Perhaps we should take this to mean that he was at the time too fully preoccupied with the new work that appeared in 1956 and that some critics of rank and renown have called his masterpiece whereas others regard it as marking a disappointing step backward. We refer to the short novel *La Chute*, which, to be sure, did show Camus in a totally new perspective.

We have here the confession of a man who once was an attorney of renown in Paris, who for years had represented to society all the high and highest civic virtues incarnate. One evening, walking across the Pont des Arts, he heard laughter somewhere behind him and felt certain that he himself was being laughed at. No one knew of his concealed guilt. Three years ago he had neglected to prevent the suicide of a woman who threw herself from one of the bridges over the Seine into the water below. For the next few days he refrained from reading the newspapers, and the pressure of his day-to-day work did its share to help him dissipate his remorse. Only the anonymous laughter so long after the event was able to penetrate to the core of his guilt and to bring him once again face to face with it. The attorney Jean-Baptiste Clamence renounces all the undeserved, lie-ridden honors heaped upon him by the Parisian society and moves to Amsterdam, where he establishes himself in the former Jewish ghetto in order to strive henceforth to be of help to the poor, the outlawed, the ambiguous creatures of life. He calls himself a "juge-pénitent," using a title invented by Camus and renderable in English only as "judge penitent." It signifies that Clamence is now a man who simultaneously passes judgment and does penance, whereas in the past he was exclusively concerned with the judging. An accidental encounter with another Frenchman in a dubious public house in Amsterdam then leads to the judge penitent's detailed confession, which we are invited to read.

This stylistically most relaxed of Camus' writings —and yet the most deliberately conscientious in its style—can give the superficial reader an impression of easy improvisation. But in reality there is hardly another work left us by Camus that could equal *La Chute* in psychological and logical condensation and continuity. If Camus tended on the whole to cultivate a somewhat elevated and at times rhetorical style, in *La Chute* he achieved a stylistic ease and, parallel to it, a totally uncontrived structural unity that had not previously been within his reach.

Clamence the judge penitent embodied for Camus, not unlike Meursault or Sisyphus, a definite idea. This idea is a far-reaching relativization of the concepts of guilt and innocence, implying that the socially irreproachable bear an inevitable trace of immorality and, conversely, the allegedly immoral have a possible grain of nonconformist morality. *La Chute* is the inexorable statement of a man who, having achieved self-knowledge, no longer brooks self-deceit and proceeds to draw the necessary consequences from his self-knowledge. Clamence pursues his confession bcause it affords him "the double pleasure of being what he is and of feeling a delightful repentance." [10] To be sure, there can be no acquittal for him, but since he does not care to live without pleasure, he enjoys the unmasking of his guilt, with narcissistic irony. And the conclusion of this confession is also suitably ironical.

The particular artistic appeal of this work lies not least in the continuous shuttling between fact and reflection. The "partner" in this conversation, about whom we learn nothing specific, becomes increasingly imaginary as we become more aware of the vagueness of his existence. All this serves only to make Clamence's spoken word more impressive in its eerie realism. And finally there is the setting, for which Camus chose in

this case a city of the north, a city of water and fog
where—to a man hailing, as did Camus, from the Mediterranean—there can be no relief for a tormented human soul. Clamence, too, is a man of the absurd—not
one who rebels but one who does penance. That is a new
element in the work of Camus, an important turn that
leads—through ironical detours and distortions—if not
to Christian tenets, at least to Christian ciphers. Would
Camus have gone on in this direction? There is no
answer to this question, but at least the possibility, it
seems to me, cannot simply be dismissed.

La Chute was to be the first in a collection of novellas which Camus planned to publish under the title
L'Exil et le royaume. This strange title seems to suggest
the author's intent. What is involved is the lives and
destinies of individual human beings living in exile,
that is to say, in Camus' view, the lives and destinies of
human beings enmeshed in situations that make it impossible for them to achieve fulfillment or to impart
meaning to the fact that they exist. They all have been
banished from a meaningful life and merely perform
their various functions as a mechanical routine. They
long for a "new kingdom" in which they might be pillar
and pivot, but in no case do we learn from Camus to
what extent the individuals do achieve their purpose in
the end. These are in a sense narrative allegories rather
than novellas, since a strict definition would require
that a novella include more pronounced climaxes in the
external events. Here, in each of these six studies, the
climactic points lie buried in silence within those who
experience them so that, externally, little happens to the

characters and even less is changed in them. They differ in concentration and in the cogency of what they can mean to us, but they are all worthy of a more penetrating analysis.

The very first of the six novellas, *L'Adultère*, is possibly the most impressive, for its action is the briefest, with very little direct discourse. And yet, when we reach the conclusion, we somehow feel that it has been a long time since we were last given an opportunity to look as deeply into a human being as we have seen into the soul of this woman, whose husband takes her along on a business trip to southern Algeria, where—in the face of the immeasurably vast desert landscape the like of which she had never seen before—she receives, as though by grace, a new inner equilibrium. She is an adulteress in the sense that she gives herself to the night, not to another man. The preparation for this, worked out by Camus through a mere exchange of glances with a French soldier in a bus, the lingering echo of the experience through which this woman "finds the way back to her roots," can only be described as a superb masterpiece of realism by intimation.

"She only knew that this kingdom had been promised her from the beginning of time and that yet it would not be hers, never, never, except perhaps for this fleeting moment when she opened her eyes on the sky which suddenly stood still and on the waves of light which suddenly appeared congealed, while abruptly the voices coming up from the Arabic settlement fell silent. It seemed to her that the world had come to a halt in its course so that from now on no one could grow older, no

one would die. Henceforth life everywhere would be
suspended, except in her heart, where at that very moment someone wept for painful astonishment." [11]

In *Les Muets* this exchange of silences as bearers
of friendly and unfriendly thoughts is likewise far more
important than all direct utterances, being endowed
with an articulateness that is more convincing than
words ever could be. A group of workmen, first and
foremost among them the forty-year-old Yvars, grumble
in wordless silence because their request for a wage in-
crease has been rejected. But then, still in brooding silence but almost put to shame, they continue their work
when human sorrow descends on their master, that is to
say, when their disrupted solidarity is reestablished on
a human basis with renewed and increased strength.
Thanks to Camus' concise and restrained technique of
summarizing, all this is not only unsurpassed in its
credibility, it is unforgettable. No less so is the novella
L'Hôte. It takes place during the time of the Algerian
war. A gendarme takes an Arab, who has been put in
chains because he has murdered a relative of his, to the
schoolmaster Daru of a remote mountain village and
asks Daru to take the prisoner to a nearby town the following day and deliver him into the hands of the law.
But Daru takes his "guest" only to the nearest cross-
roads, telling him to decide for himself whether he
should choose the road to town or the other to a camp of
nomads, which would mean freedom for him. The Arab
chooses the road leading to the town.

"A little later, standing at the window of his class-
room, the teacher watched and yet did not see the young

light leap from the heights of the heavens over the entire surface of the plateau. In back of him, on the blackboard, between the meandering courses of the rivers of France still appeared spread out, as an unskilled hand had traced it out in chalk, the inscription which a moment ago he had read: 'You have handed over our brother. For this you will pay.' Daru looked at the sky, at the plateau, and, beyond, at the invisible lands stretching out to the sea. In this vast country, which he had loved so much, he was alone." [12]

A more absurd, and yet more tragic, misunderstanding among men can hardly be imagined. Something similar could be said about *Jonas ou L'Artiste au travail*. In this novella, or at least in its ending, Camus seems to suggest that the artist has a right to his own solitary kingdom. Jonas is a successful painter, condemned in the end through his family ties and evergrowing social obligations to a life of artistic infertility. When finally in his despair he sets up a study for himself in a section of the attic, he falls ill. All that is found up there is a canvas with no painting on it but just the word *"solitaire"* or *"solidaire"* (the illegible handwriting makes it difficult to decide which).

La Pierre qui pousse is likewise filled with skepticism. Here the action occurs in the Brazilian primeval forest, where a French engineer has the assignment to build a dam. During a popular festival he watches a native who tries to carry a heavy stone to the church in fulfillment of a vow he has made. The engineer sees that the load is too heavy for the man, takes it from him, and carries it back to the native's hut. Once again Camus makes clear where he believes men have their only chance of finding happiness.

Le Renégat dissects with exaggerated, almost cruel lucidity the problems inherent in Christian missions. The novella is neither more nor less than the monologue of a Catholic missionary whom the natives have taken prisoner. After cutting out his tongue, they force him to pray to their fetish. He allows himself to be converted to evil and in the end actually kills his successor. This eerie cycle stresses once again Camus' urgent insistence that man must not look for happiness anywhere but in the realms of men and that happiness will always be of this world. Everything else leads to disaster and murder.

The thought of murder and its prevention remained a preeminent concern of Camus up to the time of his very last published works. More than anything else, he wanted to be an advocate, a protagonist of life.

Two months after the appearance of *L'Exil et le royaume,* Camus published a book, in collaboration with Arthur Koestler and Jean Bloch-Michel, entitled *Réflexions sur la peine capitale* in which Camus' contribution bore the separate title of *Réflexions sur la guillotine.* As was his wont with all problems that moved him deeply, in discussing the institution of capital punishment Camus strove to get to the very root of the matter. He remembered from his childhood that his mother had told him that his father had long ago been present at an execution and that the horror of this experience had haunted him to the end of his life. The abundance of heart-rending events which Camus had witnessed during the years of the resistance may have strengthened his convictions in this matter, enabling him to subscribe wholeheartedly to Koestler's statement that "capital punishment is a disgrace branding our society. Its advocates cannot justify it on rational grounds." [13] Camus denied the validity of the much-used argument that capital punishment functions as a deterrent. He called it "administrative murder" [14] and insisted that the true motive behind the institution of capital punishment is revenge. According to his argument, capital punishment deprives the guilty of every possibility of attempting to make restitution. He arrived at the conclusion that only a society of absolute innocence has the right to condemn a criminal to death, and such a society, obviously, does not exist.

We may emphasize, as Camus did himself, that he was not guided in this case by humanitarian considerations. The overworked concept of humanitarianism, which often hides sheer sentimentality and lack of character, was suspect to Camus. What induced him to take a clear stand against capital punishment was, as he put it, "reasons of rational pessimism, of logic, and of realism." And it was only in an aside that he conceded that it would be wrong to insist "that the heart has no part in what I have said." [15]

We do not know what induced the Royal Swedish Academy, on October 17, 1957, to award the Nobel Prize for literature to Albert Camus. The news came as a great surprise to all the world and most of all to Camus himself. Never before had so relatively young an author been given this highest literary distinction the world has to offer. In his case the Nobel Prize brought world-wide fame, whereas with most of his predecessors the sequence had been the reverse: the prize had come as a result and, perhaps, as a confirmation of their world renown.

Certainly Camus—as the official justification issued by the Academy put it—had, "in penetrating earnest, drawn attention to the problems confronting the conscience of mankind in our day," [16] but is it not true that numerous other writers had done the same? I am inclined to think that here the jury was guided by its healthy concern for the outstanding ethical personality —which it considered equal in significance with the man's intellectual achievements. To be sure, this was not universally recognized at the time. There was no lack, in France or elsewhere, of envy or of honest discontent. As for Camus himself, one has the impression that his initial sense of surprise soon came to be mingled with a certain embarrassment, and then there was also the fact that for weeks on end his incoming mail increased in bulk a hundredfold, while he was thirsting for rest and quiet in order to be able to pursue new projects. He was working on his first broadly conceived novel, *Le Premier homme*, which was never completed and of which no fragments have so far been published.

Many of Camus' friends thought that the early distinction of the Nobel Prize might hinder rather than further him in his artistic development. There is no reason to agree with this view, even though it is true that now for the first time in his life Camus could feel relieved of all financial worries. He purchased a country house in Lourmarin not far from Avignon in the northern part of Provence, where he intended to spend six months of every year in productive seclusion. The rest of the year would be spent in Paris, since he had meanwhile come to regard it as one of life's greatest distinctions to live there. But he was able to enjoy the privilege of commuting on this schedule between Paris and his country home for only two years. During the winter of 1959–1960 the Herbert Company was touring all of France and part of Switzerland with Camus' stage version of *The Demons*. Plans had been completed for extending the tour to North Africa, and Camus was to travel with the company. Before doing so he still had to take care of a few obligations that made it necessary for him to go to Paris. He did not get there. The car in which he was traveling smashed at high speed into a tree by the roadside when one of its tires blew out. Camus was killed instantly. The day was January 4, 1960, a day of mourning for the entire civilized world.

We cannot take leave of him more fittingly than by letting him speak to us once again of what he regarded as the highest mission of the creative artist. In his acceptance speech on having been awarded the Nobel Prize for literature he stated on December 10, 1957, at the city hall of Stockholm:

"As I see it, art is not a solitary enjoyment. It is a means to move great numbers of people by giving them an exquisite image of shared suffering and joy. It thus obliges the artist not to isolate himself. It makes him subservient to the most humble and most universal truth. And he who has chosen the life of an artist—as often occurs—because he believes himself different will soon learn that he can nurture his art and his difference only by avowing his resemblance to all men. The artist is formed through this perpetual give and take between himself and others, halfway between beauty which he cannot let go and the community of men from which he cannot tear himself away. It is for this reason that the true artist despises nothing. He feels it to be his duty to understand and not to judge. And, if in this world he must take sides, he can side only with a society in which, in accordance with Nietzsche's great word, it is not the judge but the creator that rules, regardless of whether he be a workman or an intellectual.

"By implication, the role of the writer cannot be separated from grave duties. By definition, he cannot in this day place himself at the service of those who make history; he is at the service of those who endure it." [17]

Chronology

1913: November 7, born in Mondovi (Algeria).

1914: Death of Camus' father in the Battle of the Marne. His mother, with both her children, moves to Algiers-Belcourt.

1918: Camus enters elementary school at Belcourt.

1923: Admission to the Lycée of Algiers.

1930: First attack of tuberculosis.

1931: Begins university studies.

1932: Baccalaureate.

1933: Camus' first marriage. He takes up various activities in order to make a living.

1934: Divorce. Membership in the Communist Party.

1935: Camus leaves the Communist Party. Founding of the *Théâtre du Travail*. Cooperative work on the play *Révolte dans les Asturies*.

1936: Camus submits his essay *Métaphysique chrétienne et néoplatonisme* for the *Diplôme d'études supérieures*.

1936: Reasons of health prevent Camus from taking his oral examination. His first literary work is brought out by the publisher Charlot: *L'Envers et l'endroit*.

111

1938:   Recovery in Savoy and travel to Florence. Second
        publication, again with Charlot: *Noces*. Camus writes
        his first drama: *Caligula*. Staging of *The Brothers
        Karamazov* at the *Théâtre de l'Equipe*. Through the
        mediation of Pascal Pia, editor-in-chief of the news-
        paper *Alger Républicain*, Camus begins to work as a
        journalist for that publication.

1939:   *Le Minotaure ou la halte d'Oran* (essay). Series of
        articles on social conditions among the Kabyles.
        Camus begins work on *L'Etranger*.

1940:   Second marriage. Camus is forced to leave Algeria
        and goes to Paris to work at the editorial offices of
        Paris-Soir. Completes *L'Etranger*. After the arrival of
        the German troops he moves to Lyons and intermit-
        tently Clermont-Ferrand. Begins composition of *Le
        Mythe de Sisyphe*.

1941:   Completion of *Le Mythe de Sisyphe*.

1942:   Publication of *L'Etranger* with the Gallimard imprint.
        Camus joins the resistance group "Combat." *Le Mythe
        de Sisyphe* is published.

1943:   *Combat*, the underground publication of the resist-
        ance group of the same name, sends Camus to Paris,
        where he works simultaneously as a reader for Galli-
        mard. The first *Lettre à un ami allemand* appears in
        Combat.

1944:   The three additional letters to a German friend are
        ready. Premiere of Camus' second play, *Le Malen-
        tendu*. Liberation of Paris. Camus begins writing edi-
        torials for *Combat*.

1945:   Premiere of his first drama, *Caligula*.

1946:   Camus' trip to the United States of America.

1947:   Camus leaves the editorial offices of *Combat*. Publica-
        tion of the novel *La Peste*. Prix des Critiques.

1948:   Premiere of Camus' third drama, *L'Etat de siège*.

1949:   Trip to South America. Premiere of his fourth drama,
        Les Justes.

1950:   Work on his philosophical book, *L'Homme révolté*.

1951: Publication of *L'Homme révolté*.

1952: Camus breaks off relations with UNESCO.

1953: Substitute director of the theatrical festivals in Angers. Two independent productions.

1954: New edition of *L'Envers et l'endroit;* also a series of more recent essays, *L'Eté*.

1955: Trip to Greece. Takes a stand on the problem of Algeria in the newspaper *L'Express*.

1956: Publication of *La Chute*. Camus appeals to his fellow writers to approach the United Nations on behalf of Hungary.

1957: Publication of *L'Exil et le royaume.* Camus is awarded the Nobel Prize for literature.

1958: Camus' collected articles on the problem of Algeria, written since 1939, are published under the title *Chroniques algériennes*.

1959: Premiere of Camus' stage adaptation of Dostoevski's *The Demons*. Begins work on a new novel, *Le Premier homme*.

1960: January 4, killed in an automobile accident.

Bibliographical References

All the quotations in the text are translations based on volumes 161 and 183 of the *Bibliothèque de la Pléiade* (Gallimard), that is, Albert Camus, *Théâtre, récits, nouvelles,* and Albert Camus, *Essais,* referred to below as I and II, respectively. The individual works by Camus that are discussed in the text, all contained in I or II, are the following*:

Caligula (Caligula)
Le Malentendu (Cross Purpose)
L'Etat de siège [State of Siege]
Les Justes (The Just Assassins)
Révolte dans les Asturies [Revolt in Asturias]
Pierre de Larivey: *Les Esprits* [The Spirits]
Pedro Calderón de la Barca: *La Dévotion à la croix* [Devotion to the Cross]
Dino Buzzati: *Un Cas intéressant* [A Clinical Case]

*The English titles in parentheses are those of works published in translation. For works not published in translation, English titles have been supplied in brackets.

Lope de Vega: *Le Chevalier d'Olmedo* [The Caballero of Olmedo]

William Faulkner: *Requiem pour une nonne* (Requiem for a Nun)

Dostoevski: *Les Possédés* (The Demons; The Possessed)

L'Etranger (The Stranger; The Outsider)

La Peste (The Plague)

La Chute (The Fall)

L'Exil et le royaume (Exile and the Kingdom)
>   *La Femme adultère*
>   *Le Renégat ou un esprit confus*
>   *Les Muets*
>   *L'Hôte*
>   *Jonas ou l'Artiste au travail*
>   *La Pierre qui pousse*

L'Envers et l'endroit [Right Side, Wrong Side]
>   *Préface*
>   *L'Ironie*
>   *Entre oui et non*
>   *La Mort dans l'âme*
>   *Amour de vivre*
>   *L'Envers et l'endroit*

Noces [Nuptials]
>   *Noces à Tipasa*
>   *Le Vent à Djémila*
>   *L'Eté à Alger*
>   *Le Désert*

Le Mythe de Sisyphe (The Myth of Sisyphus)

Lettres à un ami allemand [Letters to a German Friend]

Actuelles I, chroniques 1944–1948 (Resistance, Rebellion, and Death)

L'Homme révolté (The Rebel)

Actuelles II, chroniques 1948–1953 (Resistance, Rebellion, and Death)

L'Eté [Summer]
>   *Le Minotaure ou la Halte d'Oran*
>   *Les Amandiers*

Prométhée aux enfers
L'Enigme
Retour à Tipasa
La Mer au plus près
Actuelles III, chroniques algériennes 1939–1958 (Resistance,
　Rebellion, and Death)
Réflexions sur la guillotine [On Capital Punishment]
Discours de Suède (Speech of Acceptance)

Notes

1. *The Source*

    1. *Amour de vivre* (II, 44, 25).
    2. *Entre oui et non* (II, 25, 5).
    3. *L'Envers et l'endroit* (Preface, II, 7, 18).
    4. *L'Envers et l'endroit* (Preface, II, 6, 24).
    5. *L'Envers et l'endroit* (Preface, II, 7, 20).
    6. *L'Eté à Alger* (II, 72, 7).
    7. Press release (I, 1688, 5).

2. *In the Foothills of Knowledge*

    1. *L'Envers et l'endroit* (Preface, II, 11, 8).
    2. *L'Envers et l'endroit* (Preface, II, 9, 37).
    3. *L'Envers et l'endroit* (Preface, II, 10, 7).
    4. *L'Ironie* (II, 18, 16).
    5. *L'Ironie* (II, 22, 19).
    6. *Entre oui et non* (II, 24, 31).

7. *Entre oui et non* (II, 27, 11).
8. *La Mort dans l'âme* (II, 35, 23).
9. *La Mort dans l'âme* (II, 38, 30).
10. *La Mort dans l'âme* (II, 39, 12).
11. *La Mort dans l'âme* (II, 39, 28).
12. *Amour de vivre* (II, 42, 32).
13. *Amour de vivre* (II, 42, 33).
14. *Amour de vivre* (II, 44, 23).
15. *L'Envers et l'endroit* (II, 47, 16).
16. *L'Envers et l'endroit* (II, 49, 32).
17. *Noces à Tipasa* (II, 56, 14).
18. *Noces à Tipasa* (II, 57, 20).
19. *Noces à Tipasa* (II, 58, 10).
20. *Le Vent à Djémila* (II, 63, 22).
21. *Le Vent à Djémila* (II, 64, 21).
22. *Le Vent à Djémila* (II, 65, 20).
23. *L'Eté à Alger* (II, 75, 18).
24. *L'Eté à Alger* (II, 76, 9).
25. *Le Désert* (II, 88, 27).
26. *Le Désert* (II, 80, 31).

3. *The World of the Absurd*

1. *Le Mythe de Sisyphe* (II, 100, 18).
2. *The Stranger* (Preface, American edition, I, 1920, 30).
3. *L'Etranger* (I, 1166, 21).
4. *L'Etranger* (I, 1204, 1).
5. *L'Etranger* (I, 1209, 43).
6. *The Stranger* (Preface, American edition, I, 1920, 6).
7. *Le Mythe de Sisyphe* (II, 197, 35).
8. *Le Mythe de Sisyphe* (II, 198, 17).
9. *Le Mythe de Sisyphe* (II, 196, 41).
10. *Le Mythe de Sisyphe* (II, 111, 20).
11. *Le Mythe de Sisyphe* (II, 111, 32).

12. *Le Mythe de Sisyphe* (II, 112, 29).
13. *Le Mythe de Sisyphe* (II, 139, 24).
14. *Lettres à un ami allemand* (II, 243, 20).
15. *Lettres à un ami allemand* (II, 219, 9).
16. *L'Etranger* (I, 1180, 19).

4. *Resistance*

1. *La Peste* (I, 1425, 22).
2. *La Peste* (I, 1213, 1).
3. *La Peste* (I, 1294, 16).
4. *La Peste* (I, 1951, 17).
5. *La Peste* (I, 1395, 40).
6. *La Peste* (I, 1321, 9).
7. *La Peste* (I, 1321, 40).
8. *L'Homme révolté* (II, 423, 1).
9. *L'Homme révolté* (II, 652, 17).
10. *L'Homme révolté* (II, 647, 16).
11. *L'Homme révolté* (II, 707, 34).
12. *L'Homme révolté* (II, 641, 36).
13. *Les Possédés* (Press release, I, 1877, 28).

5. *Light Regained*

1. *Retour à Tipasa* (II, 874, 18).
2. *L'Envers et l'endroit* (Preface, II, 13, 16).
3. *L'Envers et l'endroit* (Preface, II, 10, 31).
4. *L'Enigme* (II, 865, 23).
5. *Retour à Tipasa* (II, 871, 27).
6. *Retour à Tipasa* (II, 872, 35).
7. *Retour à Tipasa* (II, 875, 39).
8. *Retour à Tipasa* (II, 876, 5).
9. *La Mer au plus près* (II, 886, 33).
10. *La Chute* (I, 1546, 35).
11. *La Femme adultère* (I, 1568, 28).

12. *L'Hôte* (I, 1621, 40).

13. *Réflexions sur la guillotine* (II, 1024, 10).

14. *Réflexions sur la guillotine* (II, 1031, 5).

15. *Réflexions sur la guillotine* (II, 1062, 6).

16. *Discours de Suède* (II, 1893, 12).

17. *Discours de Suède* (II, 1071, 32).